Still,
Tougher Than Woodpecker Lips

By

Al Rudolph

Still, Tougher Than Woodpecker Lips
by Al Rudolph

Printed in the United States of America

ISBN 9781609574604

www.xulonpress.com

Testimonial Page

Al's first book, **Tougher Than Woodpecker Lips** gave us several practical suggestions on developing traits necessary to survive in our world. **Still, Tougher Than Woodpecker Lips** provides even more insights, more practical guidance on how not only to survive, but to excel in our daily lives. "Tougher" is good, but to be "Still Tougher" is even better. This is a very enjoyable read on a very important topic - everyday life.

John K. Layer, Ph. D, P.E.
Director and Assistant Professor
University of Evansville

It is not often that a book is written that offers so many life lessons. I have created classroom icebreaker exercises, classroom devotions and entire lectures around the chapters in Al Rudolph's books. I make this recommended reading for all my students and business associates. I highly suggest **Still, Tougher Than Woodpecker Lips** for everyone and am confident they will discover the wonder of scripture as it relates to our own life.

Steve Overbey
Indiana Wesleyan University
Art Institute of Indianapolis
President, SMS Marketing Co.

"He's done it again! Al Rudolph's **Still Tougher Than Woodpecker Lips** is a hit! The forty different subject matters that Al presents in this inspiring book will not only impart wisdom…they'll put spring in your steps. An amazingly simple book that will bless anyone who reads it!"

Dru Ashwell
Executive Editor, College Press Publishing
Professor, Ozark Christian College

Acknowledgements

It would be impossible to acknowledge all the people who have helped me through the years. However, I would be remiss if I allowed that to prevent me from mentioning some who deserve recognition for shaping who I am today. First and foremost is my beautiful and wonderful wife, Linda. She has supported me and encouraged me through our 41 years of marriage and given my life meaning when the world offered none. She was the driving force in my coming to accept Jesus Christ as my Lord and Savior, and for that I am *eternally* grateful. Her love has been and continues to be the driving force in my daily walk, and I look forward to each day with her by my side as we do life together.

And where would I be without the love and support of our lovely and talented daughter Stephanie? She has always been a fan of mine, even when I seemed to strike out in life (and fatherhood). I know I wasn't there for her as much as I should have been during her growing years as I allowed work to steal some of my time from her, but she developed into a beautiful independent person of integrity in spite of my shortcomings. Stephanie, I hope you never lose your love for adventure and your love for life, and thanks for giving meaning to mine.

Being the youngest of twelve children, I need to thank each of my brothers and sisters who helped raise and nurture me with love and support through all my years. And the family I inherited by marrying Linda has also been a blessing to me. Family means more to me than I ever take time to admit.

While speaking of family, I am blessed beyond measure to be a part of the First Capital Christian Church family and the Dayspring Emmaus family. Both supply me with love, joy, peace, patience, kindness, goodness, faithfulness, gentleness and help me with self-control. To each of you, "Thanks" for putting up with me, and for keeping me on the straight and narrow path as much as possible. I look forward to our days together, whether they are here on earth or visiting each other at our mansions prepared for us in Heaven. Either way, I am blessed because of you!

And to my fellow Toastmasters, not only at the Sunnyside Club, but to all the clubs I have had the privilege of taking part in through the past 25 years, I appreciate the positive, constructive feedback you have supplied in helping me develop my public speaking skills. I can only hope I have contributed a fraction of the encouraging words to each of you that you have given me. Raise your glass and give yourselves a toast!

Randy West gets a special bit of gratitude for his skill in editing my words and for shaping them to a much better form that I could have done. You make my thoughts more appetizing by adding your own special brand of flavor and spice. *Bon appetite!*

Thanks to Joe Kellum for his efforts in getting the cover of the book to its eye-appealing point. His computer skills never cease to amaze me, and the way he can take a simple idea and bring it to life is amazing. Keep up the good work!

Once again I must recognize Steve and Carolyn Wood who so graciously opened their home to me on the banks of the Tennessee River, in the friendly town of Saltillo, Tennessee. And long before they opened their home, they opened their hearts and welcomed me in as a friend. I am always in awe at the way this couple can make anyone feel at home in their presence. I can only hope to have some of their generosity and hospitality rub off on me so I, too, can make a difference in others lives, *here and now*.

To each and every one who honored me by buying and reading my first book, **Tougher Than Woodpecker Lips**, I am forever grateful. I hope you were enlightened and entertained, and if you happened to find a thought or two that spoke to you, may you be willing to share them with someone else. If you found no joy at all, then do yourself a favor and forget this one, because it is filled with more of the same! To those of you brave enough to go for a second helping, pull up a chair and grab yourself a cup of your favorite beverage and kick back, knowing that some times life is **Still, Tougher Than Woodpecker Lips!**

Al Rudolph

Table of Contents

~:~

Foreword

ᵕ∵∼

What's down in the well comes out in the bucket! And so it is with the wit and wisdom found in **Still, Tougher Than Woodpecker Lips.** Each chapter gives a glimpse of Al Rudolph's mind (That's a scary thought!), but more than that, his heart. You can learn a lot about a man when you read what he has put to print.

Al likes people. He watches; he notices how we think and what makes us tick. He identifies the issues that concern us and the topics that stir us. He knows a good story and how to tell it. He knows people.

Reading **Still, Tougher Than Woodpecker Lips** you soon realize Al knows himself. You get a sense of Al's personality. Quick, no wasted time, organized, efficient – his words are carefully chosen and the pace is brisk. Its short chapters make it a "potato chip" read – you can't stop with just one! But the insights are keen; you can stop at any point you've found a principle you want to contemplate and come back for another day. You can sense his enjoyment in the little things of life, his ability to pick life's lessons from the ordinary pieces of every day.

There are some people – you don't need to be around them very long to recognize – who know Jesus on a first-name basis. That's Al. He couldn't hide it if he tried; but he doesn't try. His faith peeks through on every page. It would be easy to think this book is about principles, or people, but it's not. It's all about one man's relationship with the One Man who forever changed him.

Bring a bookmark and a pen when you sit down to read this one. Mark up your copy. Underline, write a note in the margin. You might even dog ear a page or two. The bookmark is so you can stop, hold that thought, walk away and chew on it a while. Then come back and snack on another "chip" or two. Enjoy yourself.

Randy Kirk
Al's minister, friend and fellow soldier in the Lord's Army

Introduction

For those of you who took the time to read my first book, **Tougher Than Woodpecker Lips**, I say, *"Welcome back!"* If this is your first visit to my writings, I say, *"Welcome."*

Still, Tougher Than Woodpecker Lips is a collection of another forty short chapters on different issues that I believe need to be a part of our everyday routine as we live in this world. I feel these can and will make a positive difference if we just take the time to ponder them and put them into practice in our lives. As with my first book, this one also touches mostly on aspects that we would benefit from having as part of our daily living (good communication, loyalty, patience, etc.), as well as a few things that we need to be leery of (stress, procrastination, laziness, etc.) in order to keep them at bay.

If there is one thing I have discovered in my life it is that sometimes things just don't go the way we would prefer, and if we are not careful, we will become discouraged and feel like giving up. There is not a person out there who has not felt this sometime in their life, and it is not something to be ashamed of. We just need to admit that life is tough, and know that we can be **"Still, Tougher Than Woodpecker Lips,"** and come out the victor. As you read, consider how you might apply these thoughts to become a part of who you are, as you proceed in becoming the person you want to be and that God created you to be.

If you find any fault in my words, blame me. If you should find any praise for them, tell Him and praise Him, for they are thoughts He blessed me with. And never forget that no matter how much the world at large and our world in particular may seem to be out of control, they are not. God is in control! Thanks be to Him.

I Think I Can, I Think I Can!

Having ability is important, but being convinced that you are capable of fulfilling the role at hand with that ability is more than a small portion of getting the job done. The other thing that plays an important part in getting a job done is to be available when an opportunity presents itself. For if you are not available, someone less gifted will do the job, and something less than what is possible may be the result. Ability, attitude and availability are the trio that makes tasks possible. The little train that thought it could was there when the hill presented itself, had the mind set that it could get over the hill, and used every ounce of its ability to prove itself. When we do the same, we, too, can utter those famous words from the children's classic, *"I think I can, I think I can."*

Do not judge the strength of the world by the weakness you possess. However, do not underestimate your strength in developing those weaknesses to the world's standards and beyond. Natural ability, even unschooled, can raise one to greater heights than the most educated, with education alone. When our ability is tested, it gives us an opportunity to improve.

**"Do not judge the strength of the world
by the weakness you possess."**

Ability alone will never be anything more than what it is, but when mixed with sincere enthusiasm and support from others, the sky is the limit. It can be a dangerous lot to expect more from a person than their ability allows. However, in that danger also lays the possibility of newfound skills. Your ability grows when exercised; however, it dies a slow death if left unchallenged. But we must keep in mind that it is not wise to give a saw to one who only knows how to use a hammer because the results will be less than desired.

To see ability in others, and have the ability to get them to the point of seeing it in themselves, is ability at its best. Everyone should be so blessed as to have someone in their lives who will believe in them enough to help them realize their full ability. Ability decreases in the presence of doubt, and increases in the presence of inspiration. No one has the ability to do all things well, but everyone has the capacity to excel in at least one thing. If I do not prompt you to become all you can be, I do a great injustice not only to you, but to myself as well. Use your ability to its fullest, and you will discover it has grown the next time you go to use it, from the experience you allowed it to enjoy.

All men are created equal; however, not all have the same levels of ability. Just as God has given different talents to each one, so have the levels of ability differed. Nevertheless, it is not what we have been given that is important, but to what level of capacity have we developed them? Many a man has a much higher opinion of his ability than what he has proven by his actions. However, little ability teamed with trying is much more productive than idle talent.

"All men are created equal; however not all have the same level of ability."

If we are willing to acknowledge our strengths and weaknesses, and work on improving both, we can lead a rich life of fulfillment. Many are those who discover they can by thinking they can. Our ability is largely shaped by the thoughts we permit to surround it. The desire to improve one's ability is a prerequisite to doing so.

Your willingness to give your all, no matter if you get the credit or not, is an ability that will not go unrewarded. Having the talent and ability to do a job well, will, in many instances, mean more to you than what you earned in doing it. Develop the talent you have to the best of your ability, and the world will reward you for it.

Do not be ashamed to step aside and allow someone who is more gifted to do a job at which you struggle. However, in stepping aside you must realize that a new challenge will now await you, even if it is simply playing second fiddle. Still, you must give it your all and do the best you can. We should never allow the fact that we cannot do something to stop us from doing all we can. No matter if you know all the words or not, sing to the best of your ability!

Just because someone states what sounds like a fact does not make it a fact. If someone says that you cannot do something, do not allow that statement to prevent you from going for it. When given the opportunity, use your ability to prove the under-evaluation of your talents as false. To place limitations on your self or on others prevents abilities from becoming able-bodied. Practice and perfect practice can transform a weakling into a tower of power.

What one begins with is of little matter, but the worth of the end product will determine how well your ability has served you. If you truly believe in your level of skill, and have the initiative to implement it, your world can be conquered. Ability and ambition working together make for success in whatever you attempt. To know your level of output equaled your highest level of ability gives a person a sense of well being, and the will to say, *"I think I can, I think I can!"*

*****

"Again, it will be like a man going on a journey, who called his servants and entrusted his property to them. To one he gave five talents of money, to another two talents, and to another one talent, each according to his ability." [Matthew 25:14-15]

Lights, Camera, Action!

I don't know if it is the teacher instinct in me or what, but I am going to give you a test. It is a simple test, but one that many people fail. It consists of one question and one question only. Ready? Here goes: *There are five birds sitting on a wire and three of them decide to fly away. How many birds are left?* Take your time and think before you answer. Let me repeat it and give you time for more thought because I really do want you to get it right. *There are five birds sitting on a wire and three of them decide to fly away. How many birds are left?*

What is your answer? Did you say *"Two"* like so many people do? Well, the correct answer is *"Five."* Now you may be saying, "Wait just a minute. Where did you go to school? Everybody knows that five minus three equals two!" And you know what? I couldn't agree with you more. But just because three of the birds *"decide"* to fly away doesn't mean they did. They must take **action** on their decision before their circumstance changes.

The same is true with each of us. We may have the best intention of doing something, but until we take action, it is of little or no use for us to have had the thought. So, let's proceed ahead: *"Lights, camera, action!"*

We have all heard the phrase *"Actions speak louder than words."* I think we all would agree with the truth of the statement because we know that just to mouth words is easy. But witnessing a person do something comes across more clearly and makes a bolder statement in regard to their character than the words they speak.

When you have hungry people, it is more beneficial to pass them the loaf of bread for their consumption than it is to hold it up and talk about the benefits of its ingredients. Words themselves will do nothing to satisfy the need that is present, until some action is taken to see that the need if fulfilled. Let us be people who follow through and take action to make sure needs are met. A ton of good intentions weighs less than a pound of loving action.

"A ton of good intentions weighs less than a pound of loving action."

While preparing this chapter, I came across an old Chinese proverb that is worth repeating. It goes like this: *"Be not afraid of going slowly; be only afraid of standing still."* I have heard many people say that they don't do something because they know others could do it better or faster. Well, I am here to tell you that may be the case, but it should not keep you from doing what you can because we have no guarantee that the one who could do it better, will. As the proverb says, we should not be afraid of doing something with less speed than another might - just do something! Disorganized action is preferred to organized idleness!

"Disorganized action is preferred to organized idleness!"

A good plan that is acted on today is far better that the best plan that is never put into action. Being in the sales field, I have heard this advice many times: *"Plan your work and then work your plan!"* That was good counsel then, and it is still good counsel today.

I used to work for a company that had a contest to see who could come up with the best sales plan of the year. I was fortunate enough to win the contest two years in a row. However, I must tell you that I actually put the "best plan" into action only one of those two years. The results speak for themselves: I won Salesman of the Year when I worked my plan, and then I became complacent. I still had what was voted the "Best Sales Plan of the Year," but I didn't even make honorable mention the next year because I did not take the steps necessary to make the plan work. It is a law of nature that the one who acts is the one who has.

Edward Burke said, *"The only thing necessary for the triumph of evil is for good men to do nothing."* Good men have good intentions of taking steps to see that evil is done away with, but those intentions do nothing to prevent iniquity from being born. The greatest wisdom is foolishness if it is not put into action. Better to do one good deed than to dream a thousand!

"Better to do one good deed than to dream a thousand!"

If you are a person of action, don't be surprised when you are criticized by others. However, most of the times you will discover that the ones doing the complaining are the ones doing nothing. If you think right and act right, you will **be** right. Don't worry about what others may think or say.

No matter how much you hope and dream for something to happen, if you haven't taken the action steps necessary to accomplish it, don't expect it to happen. If it does, a miracle will have taken place! Action is the cure for complacency.

I love the story of the husband lounging on the sofa who said to his wife, *"I'll think about hoeing the garden in a few minutes. Right now, I'm thinking about cleaning out the garage."* I mean, how much is expected out of one person anyway?

Failure will be the end result for one who has the might to do something but lacks the will to do it. The smallest act of kindness is more powerful than the grandest of schemes that never materializes. The creed by which you live may be of interest to others, but it pales in comparison to the deeds they see you do.

Your works are a much more accurate indicator of love than your words. Plowing a field in your mind does nothing to prepare the soil for seed. As I get older, I find myself paying less attention to what people say and more to what they do because that is a more accurate indicator of their character.

"Your works are a much more accurate indicator of love than your words."

You can never hope to hit a home run until you get off the bench, step up to the plate, and swing with all your might. Some of you might be thinking, *"Yeah, **but** what happens if I strike out?"* All I can tell you is to not let your **but** get in the way of doing. And don't allow memories of past failures prevent you from taking action. If you are attempting something great, there is glory even in failing.

We need to awake from our sleep, arise from our beds, and take action on our dreams. You will never arrive someplace else unless you leave where you are. So take action now because today will be yesterday when tomorrow gets here. I know you can do it, so I will close with, *"Lights, camera, action!"*

*****

Do not be deceived: God cannot be mocked. A man reaps what he sows. [Galatians 6:7]

Reverse The Adverse And Move Forward

~:~

One doesn't have to look far to find examples of people who were able to overcome tremendous obstacles in their lives and become inspirations for those who knew them or read their stories. Some are names you might recognize from celebrity status, but others are just common folk like you and me. It's funny in a way how some people are overcome by the obstacles set in their path while others find ways to use those obstacles as steps to achieving great things. Albert Einstein once suggested that "in the middle of every difficulty lies opportunity." It would behoove us to realize that adversity is unavoidable and then make up our minds to utilize the difficulty to make us stronger. In other words, *"Reverse the adverse and move forward."*

One measure of a person is displayed by the amount of adversity it takes to discourage him or her. Adverse conditions can be the fertilizer to grow one's character, or they can be the tornado that blows one away.

Adversity causes one to think. Thinking leads to wisdom, and wisdom makes life tolerable. So, learn to tolerate adversity. We can learn in times of prosperity, but the worth of the lesson will usually pale in comparison to the one taught by adversity. It will strengthen and develop the one who stands up to hard knocks.

Just as fire refines gold, adversity refines man.

Every obstacle or adversity carries a lesson with it. As a good student, we must learn from it and be better because of it. You learn little in times of ease but much in times of difficulty. Just as fire refines gold, adversity refines man. Adversity has a way of bringing out gifts in people that times of prosperity could never reveal. Few of life's most valuable lessons are learned in times of prosperity, but many in times of hardships. Adversity causes some to break, and others to break through!

Adversity causes some to break, and others to break through!

I know we don't like to think about it, but difficulties can help us realize our full capacity if we don't allow them to knock a hole in our self-worth. Just because you may fail at a certain task, this does not determine who you are. Learn from failure, and determine in your mind not to make the same mistake again. If you do, learn from both of them, and then you haven't failed at all. We seldom welcome difficult times, but more often than not we will benefit from their visit.

Adversity plus action will equal achievement if you persevere. The truth is that many times we must be torn down before we can be built up. We need to ask ourselves, "What's the condition of my building lot?"

John R. Miller said, "If you will call your troubles experiences, and remember that every experience develops some latent force within you, you will grow vigorous and happy, however adverse your circumstances may seem to be." It was determined many years ago that the important thing is not your circumstances, but your frame of mind (attitude) as you approach obstacles. One's true character cannot be developed through a life of peace and quiet. Only through the struggles of adversity is character crafted. Today's battles lead to tomorrow's victories.

A man's worth is not determined by the stand he takes when things go his way, but by the one he takes when faced with times of difficulty. Obstacles are the building blocks of strong men and women. When a person has the proper attitude and fortitude, obstacles instill a toughness that will enable the person to stand against future difficulties. You may not be in the middle of a storm at this point in your life, but odds are you just came out of one or there is one brewing just over the next hill. Resolve not to be blown away when it comes. Times of ease do not build heroes, but times of endurance will.

It is hard to do, but when difficulties come our way, we need to make every effort to think clearly and act kindly. Our natural response is often a knee-jerk reaction, and when that happens, someone usually gets kicked. However, if we can react with kindness and in a sane manner, our witness can encourage those around us. Look for the good in all obstacles, and determine how you will be better by overcoming them. Our confidence and courage grow when we overcome.

The absence of disaster is the biggest disaster of all.

Naturally, we wish we could be exempt from facing hard times, and sometimes we're convinced the lessons we learn from difficulty are not worth the struggle and pain. It's a hard lesson to learn for sure, but the absence of disaster is the biggest disaster of all. Walt Disney reportedly said, "You may not realize it when it happens, but a kick in the teeth may be the best thing in the world for you." As we look back on times of trial, we will recognize them as times of growth. One of the greatest burdens of life is never to be burdened.

Standing on the top of a mountain is made worthwhile by overcoming the obstacles of the trail to get there. I can relate to this when I think of an experience that Linda, Stephanie and I had a few years ago as we hiked in Peru. Our ultimate goal was to hike for four full days over the narrow trails of the steep mountains and finally arrive on the morning of the fifth day at the top of fabled Machu Picchu. There were spots in the trails where we literally had to pull ourselves up by sheer strength to reach the next rock where we could rest our feet. The air was so thin and the terrain so steep that we could only take a few steps before stopping to catch a breath and regain the stamina to continue. But I must tell you, all the obstacles were forgotten at the first glimpse of the majesty of Machu Picchu, the mysterious capitol of the Incas.

There is another way to visit this wonder of the world; take a train ride to the small town at the base of the mountain and then hike a few steps up to Machu Picchu. But the people who take this option do not look at the mountain with the same intensity and respect as those of us who worked very hard at overcoming obstacles for four plus days. In my mind, the obstacles we overcame added value to the experience. Just as the case of our "conquest" of Machu Picchu, adversity can lead to achievement if we stay on path, no matter how difficult it may be.

As a kite rises against the wind, strong people rise against adversity. So the next time difficulty comes your way, remember to *reverse the adverse and move forward.*

*****

I have told you these things, so that in me you may have peace. In this world you will have trouble. But take heart! I have overcome the world! [John 16:33]

Let Me Give You Some Advice!

Don't you just hate it when somebody says, *"Let me give you some advice!"* You can rest assured that you are getting ready to get an ear full of exactly what you do not want to hear. It has been said that only a fool would take advice from no one, and even a bigger fool would take the advice of everyone. We need to be very careful when it comes to advice, both giving and receiving. Please don't misunderstand me. I am not saying that there is no "good" advice to be had, but it has been my experience that if it is "good," most people are going to keep it for themselves, not willing to share it with someone else. The best advice I can give *you* is not to offer advice! [Wait a minute. Did I just advise you on that? Well, excuuuuuuze me! I was just trying to be helpful.] Now, have a seat and *"Let me give you some advice!"*

One word of warning; you need to be careful in regard to telling another, *"Just be yourself,"* as that could spell disaster for everyone involved. And while we are on the subject of warnings, another I might offer is to be leery of offering advice in regard to something you know nothing about. Oh, the urge to appear smarter than we really are is a sure-fire way of getting ourselves in trouble.

If someone asks you to be critical in your feedback, you can be sure that he or she is really looking for praise, with an occasional sprinkling of fact. We also must remember that if someone solicits our advice in regard to a particular subject, after giving it, be indifferent as to whether or not they heed it. In other words, don't get your feelings hurt simply because someone else was not smart enough to recognize the fact that you are so wise.

Many people do not ask for advice until *after* they have already decided what they are going to do, and are either looking for someone to agree with them - or someone to blame.

Francis Bacon commented, *"He that gives good advice builds with one hand; he that gives good counsel and example builds with both; but he that gives good admonition and bad example builds with one hand and pulls down with the other."* If you do not live by the advice you offer to others, what makes you think you have a right to share it?

Advice that is given after the fact is not advice at all, just another useless comment. A Danish Proverb reads, *"Advice after injury is like medicine after death."* If we are going to be silly enough to share our thoughts, the least we can do is to make sure it is timely. You will have to search far and wide to discover a gift that is given with so much pleasure as that of advice. The problem is that even when it doesn't fit, the giver has a "no-return" policy.

"It is easy to give advice for which you will suffer no consequences."

It is easy to give advice for which you will suffer no consequences. Often, the gift of advice can cost the recipient more than the giver. And sometimes "advice" is nothing more than a "guess" dressed in its dancing outfit. It is OK to ask for other people's advice, but understand that you must decide for yourself what action is best. It has been my experience that the majority of "free advice" is worth exactly what it costs: nothing. When someone tells you something cannot be done, do not allow that to prevent you from doing it.

Parents do not be disheartened in believing your advice to your children is falling on deaf ears, because 20 years from now they will be using it on your grandchildren. Sometimes the best thing to do with advice is to pass it on to another, for it will prove to be of absolutely no use to your self.

Samuel Taylor Coleridge once advised, *"Advice is like snow; the softer it falls, the longer it dwells upon, and the deeper it sinks into the mind."* It is better to give advice than it is to scold, for one corrects while the other condemns.

There will always be some who give advice and have no clue what they are talking about. Their words will soon expose them. When a person's advice goes from what he knows to what he thinks, politely excuse yourself from the conversation. Still another Danish Proverb I believe is worth sharing is, *"He who builds to every man's advice will have a crooked house."* Advice that is given in response to a request is usually more valuable than that which is offered without solicitation, but we must be on guard with both. Oh, if we could only live our life in such a way that our advice would be a sought-after commodity.

If it costs you nothing, it is classified as advice. If you have to pay for it, that is called counseling. If you can find anything of benefit in either, now that is what we call a miracle! One bit of advice that I would like to counsel you with is this: *"Never get into a puking contest with a buzzard, 'cause you are not going to win unless you are a lot sicker than I think you are."* Now I will be the first to admit that if you could find anything of benefit in that, it is a miracle for sure!

"Be slow to offer advice and slower still in accepting it."

Be slow to offer advice and slower still in accepting it. If your competitor offers you advice, you can pretty well assume that its worth is going to be minimal at best. The one who is in deepest need of advice is the same person whose desire to receive it is the shallowest. Advice, like medicine, is easy to prescribe but hard to swallow. When offering advice, use the underwear approach: keep it brief.

Even a fool can occasionally offer some useful advice, and the wisest among us can sometimes benefit from receiving it. So, *"Let me give you some advice…"*

*****

"My son, keep your father's commands and do not forsake your mother's teaching. Bind them upon your heart forever; fasten them around your neck." [Proverbs 6:20-23]

He Is Quite A Character!

Insinuating that someone is quite a character can be a compliment or an insult, depending on what kind of a person we believe one to be. If we say it with enthusiasm and love, we could mean they are one you truly enjoy being around, and the "character" in them brings out the best in you.

On the other hand, if we say it with intent to let others know that they need to keep a close eye on the behavior of someone, and not to expect good things, it is not a compliment.

Each of us has character, and it is not something that we are born with; it develops throughout our entire lives. Your character will either draw people to you or repel them. A treasure beyond measure is a character admired by others. Your actions are nothing more than your character put on public display.

"A treasure beyond measure is a character admired by others."

Only we can be us. We cannot escape the reality of our character, for even in pretending to be something we are not, the character trait of deceit rears its ugly head. A person of noble character controls the thoughts upon which they dwell, and never allow their thoughts to take control. Character is one thing we cannot fool or run away from. If we do, it will soon overtake us again, though this time a bit weaker than before, simply from the attempt to escape.

There are certain characteristics of character that cannot be mistaken for signs of superiority; humility and sincere heart for others are but two of them. To get an accurate evaluation of a person's character, observe how they treat those who the world look at as being second class citizens. To laugh at what is funny is to know life, and shows good taste. To laugh in moments of misfortune to others shows no taste or character at all.

Being rigid and being moral may at first resemble each other; however, upon closer inspection, you will notice that one is cold and stiff, while the other is warm and flexible. If you would learn the character of a person, it would be what shows when no one else is around to see. Character doesn't change when someone is watching - the actions might, but the character does not. It is true that who we are, and who we think we are, are usually very different. Let your works speak for you, not your words. When doing what is right is more important to a person than doing what is convenient, character lives there.

The persona of personality can disguise character to appear as something it is not. Our work, and the level of commitment on our part, speaks volumes in regard to the character of our lives.

Our garden of character should have rows and rows of love, peace, patience, kindness, goodness, self-control, etc. Then the weeds of worry and selfishness will have nowhere to grow.

All aspects of a person's life are affected by what he holds to, as being worth holding onto. Clothes may make a person appear to be something they are not, but you cannot mistake a person of true character. The foundation of our character will determine the stability of the life we build on it.

"The foundation of our character will determine the stability of the life we build upon it."

One can obtain a truer perspective of a person's character in two minutes after a loss of some sort than in hours of victory celebrations.

It is impossible to go on vacation and not take your character with you. One of the scary things is that we must not only accept responsibility for the quality of character we become, but also, to a degree, how we guide and influence those around us. For, if you desire others to develop character traits, you must be intentional in setting the example for them.

Character is forged from the heat of fiery moments and hammered from the blows of battle. A crisis is not the place where character is designed but put on display. In a moment of crisis, the strength of a person's character is tested.

If our lives end up on a dead-end road, we must remember that God does allow U-turns, and we should take advantage of the situation and take the necessary steps to ensure ourselves that we do not end up there in the future.

We should live our lives in such a way that if our worst enemy hears something bad about us, even he will question its validity. If our coat of character has but one spot of dirt, that is what every eye gravitates to and ultimately focuses on. Character is something that is easier to hold onto than pick back up when it has been dropped.

Our natural tendency is to want to blame how we react to a certain situation on the circumstances that surround it. However, to blame your circumstances for flaws in your character is like yelling at the mirror for the way you look. The true beauty of one's heart should show on one's face.

"Character is forged from the heat of fiery moments and hammered from the blows of battle."

The next time someone says "You are quite a character," ask yourself just what they mean. It is my hope that they are saying it in a manner of love and respect, but, if not, do yourself and everyone else a favor. Make the U-turn and get headed in the right direction.

*****

"Not only so, but we also rejoice in our sufferings, because we know that suffering produces perseverance; perseverance, character; and character, hope." [Romans 5:3-4]

I Can't Believe You Said That!

⌣∶∾

It has been more years than I would like to admit since I have watched the movie "Cool Hand Luke," and really cannot tell you any of the dialogue except for the one classic line, *"What we have here is a failure to communicate."* Wow, how many instances have each of us had in our lives when we could have said that? If the truth were known, it could be very appropriate, daily, for some of us.

One of our problems is that the people who have something to say can't do so effectively and the ones who have nothing to say have diarrhea of the mouth. I know what some of you are thinking; *"I can't believe you said that!"* Well, one of the things that I have discovered is, for a person to be a good communicator, first, he or she must be clear to him or her self before they can be clear to others. And I can assure you that I know exactly what I was trying to say, so I am assuming you did as well.

It has been estimated that more than half of all managerial problems are the results of poor communication. In regard to issues that can lead to divorce, it has been estimated that nearly 100% can be blamed on the failure to communicate effectively. With statistics like these, it is obvious that we have some serious work to be done in honing our communication skills if we hope to survive. Communication is the oil that lubricates any relationship and keeps it running smoothly.

"Communication is the oil that lubricates any relationship, and keeps it running smoothly."

Communication is more than simply sending a message. In addition to hearing the message, it must be understood in such a way that appropriate action is taken. If people will not listen to you, at least a part of the blame is yours, due to the way you present yourself. In any communication, our area of concern needs to be that those listening get the point we are trying to make. Ideas without our ability to express them are of little or no value. The ability to express one's self is among life's most valuable assets.

Communication involves many facets, of which the spoken word is but one. For example the tone of voice, body language and gestures many times speak louder than words. When we speak of "body language" I think we would all have to agree that some are far more eloquent than others. *"Know what I mean Vern?"*

The delivery of your words also plays a vital role and may be just as important as the words themselves. One of the biggest problems in communication is trying to make sure the image produced in our hearer's mind, by our words, is equal to the image we wish them to have. When the images do not match, then we have miscommunication issues.

A good communicator knows both what to say and what not to say. Gerald Goodman once remarked, *"Silences regulate the flow of listening and talking. They are to conversations what zeros are to mathematics - crucial nothings without which communication cannot work."* The art of not speaking before the brain has had an opportunity to think is a rare art indeed. A properly placed pause speaks volumes.

"A good communicator knows both
what to say and what not to say."

Make sure your words are soft and sweet, so if you should have to eat them, they won't be so difficult to swallow. Just remember, it is almost impossible for words you never say to be used against you. As the old saying goes, *"A closed mouth gathers no foot!"* The problem with the "gift of gab" is, "How do you wrap it?"

Words are among the most powerful weapons available in the world, and, at the same time, the greatest of all peacemakers. Words are but a drug that will either sedate or invigorate, depending on how they are delivered. Sharp words can leave deep wounds and scars that last a lifetime. They can tear relationships to pieces.

Before you say something you will be sorry for, stop and think! Sometimes many words reveal few thoughts. It has been said, *"A quick tongue and a brilliant mind are never found in the same skull."* The fiercest of all animals is the man who talks even though he has nothing to say.

Oral communication is a three-step process; first is **talking**, the second is **listening,** and the third is **understanding**. The understanding part will not happen in the absence of either of the other two. Communication does not have to be lengthy to be worthwhile, only understood. It is better to speak one language in such a way that it is easy to understand, than to be fluent in a dozen with no comprehension.

"Communication does not have to be lengthy to be worthwhile, only understood."

In speaking of problems with communication and the choice of words, I'm reminded of the story about the man whose wife was out for the evening, pursuing her hobby of making porcelain dolls at a doll-making class. The husband was at home baby sitting his four-year-old son. He had his arms in the dishwater up to his elbows when the phone rang. He was quite pleased when his young son answered the phone in a prompt and polite manner. However, his pleasure soon turned to panic as he heard his young son say to the person on the other end of the line, "No, my momma's not here. She's out making a baby. But my dad's here if you want to talk to him." And as luck would have it, it was the preacher!... What can I say?

Whether we like it or not, the words we use and the eloquence we present them with is what others use to draw their conclusions about us. Moreover, it seems to be in direct correlation that the less a person thinks, the more they talk. What? Are you insinuating that you know now why I talk so much? *"I can't believe you said that!"*

*****

"My dear brothers, take note of this: Everyone should be quick to listen, slow to speak and slow to become angry." [James 1:19]

How Much Is Enough?

The story has been told of an old farmer who had grown tired of the land he lived on and finally decided to sell it. He called the real estate agent who promptly came to look at the farm so he could place an ample description of it in a local newspaper ad. Before running the ad, the agent called the farmer and read it to him over the phone, just to make sure it sounded OK. After hearing the ad, the farmer immediately told the agent that the deal was off. He said, *"I've been dreaming of a place like that for years!*

Life is like that sometimes, isn't it? We really do not realize just how blessed we are until we take the time to look at it from a different perspective.

"More than enough is too much!"

We become discontented when we take our eyes off what we have and start eyeballing what someone else has. Contentment is an "inside" job, and it's the most precious gift you can ever give yourself. It comes when you learn to enjoy what you have and lose interest in what you don't. The world will make us miserable by convincing us that having more material wealth will make us happy. We have bought into this falsehood so deeply that we sacrifice all the things that mean the most to us for things that are worth the least. It is past time for a reality check! Learn to enjoy the blessings of what you have, and you will discover the secret of contentment. Therefore, I ask you, *"How much is enough?"* More than enough is too much!

If you cannot be content with what you have, what makes you think you could be content with more? It is a fact that money cannot buy happiness, and contentment is not for sale. Among the poorest people on earth are those who cannot enjoy the simple things of life, for want of more. To have basic needs fulfilled should be enough for anyone, but most forget their needs and think only of their wants. Having a bad case of the "wants" will prevent contentment from staying at your house.

When we discover that life is a *gift* and not a *right*, we will find contentment visiting our place more often. Most people have the false idea that great wealth will bring contentment, but the truth is, contentment comes from having the basic needs and few other wants. To have one's health and to be in the company of those you love - what else could be better?

I would be remiss if I did not include a quote by Johann Wolfgang Von Goethe on the subject of contentment. *"There are nine requisites for contented life: Health enough to make work a pleasure. Wealth enough to support your needs. Strength enough to battle with difficulties and overcome them. Grace enough to confess your sins and forsake them. Patience enough to toil until some good is accomplished. Charity enough to see some good in your neighbor. Love enough to move you to be useful and helpful to others. Faith enough to make real the things of God. Hope enough to remove all anxious fears concerning the future."*

What a difference it could make in each of our lives if we had Goethe's insight where we could see it, and read it everyday.

"Contentment with what you have is a blessing. Contentment with who you are is a curse."

Contentment with what you have is a real blessing. Contentment with who you are is a curse. We should always be striving to develop the talents we have been gifted with, not necessarily to **get** more, but to be able to **give** more. Moreover, being content with your level of moral purity is never a mark of wisdom. There are always ways in which we can improve our lives, and it is our duty to search for them and make them a part of our everyday being.

A wise person will dwell more on the blessings of what he has, and less on what he has been denied. Sad indeed is the one who is so caught up in chasing after things they do not have, to find the time to enjoy the things they do. For the one who's always searching for more is a slave of the hunt. Instead of worrying about the things you do not have that you want, concentrate on all the things you don't have that you don't want. Contentment comes easier in this light.

Warning! There is a devastating epidemic spreading across our country at break-neck speed. Most of us are already infected with it and don't realize it. Only a few, who have had the insight to inoculate themselves, will be spared. The bad thing is that you can catch it by simply looking over your backyard fence and seeing the things of your neighbor. What, you dare ask, is this terrible disease? *Stuffitis!* Correct me if I am wrong, but you do have it, don't you? Well, never fear for I have saved the great news until now: you, too, can inoculate yourself from this life-sucking disease simply by realizing that you already have everything you need to be happy. Just dwell upon the good in all things and be pleased with whatever circumstances you find yourself in.

"Until we can discover contentment in ourselves, we are wasting our time looking for it elsewhere."

Learn to love life by being thankful for the miracles of each day, and be grateful for all the ills with which you are not afflicted. Until we can discover contentment in ourselves, we are wasting our time looking for it elsewhere. You will become your own best friend when you become content. Therefore, I ask you again, *"How much is enough?"*

*****

"But godliness with contentment is great gain. For, we brought nothing into the world and we can take nothing out of it. But if we have food and clothing, we will be content with that."
[1 Timothy 6:6-8]

You Know What I'd Really Like?

I think a problem that many of us have is the fact that we really do not know what it is we want.

With the possibilities seeming to have no end, there is just so much to choose from that we are afraid to pick something for fear that we might be missing out on something else. Decisions, decisions, decisions! Nevertheless, if we are ever going to decide on something, and make it our desire, we must understand that sacrifices will be required to make our desire a reality. Just because you make up your mind to achieve some lofty dream does not assure you that there will be no obstacles to overcome. However, it does assure you of the strength to survive. The fight is not over but the battle is won when the desire to win steps into the ring to face the opponent. When you desire something strongly enough to be willing to sacrifice what you now have to achieve it, you can have it. You just need to make sure it is worth what you are going to have to give up to attain it.

"If you can dream it, you can redeem it!"

"You know what I'd really like?" At the moment I am writing this, what I would really like is to be able to complete this book and get it ready for publishing. At the moment you are reading this, I will have something else that I would really like, for my previous desire will have been realized. That is one of the great things about our desires - they change as we change.

When you desire something strongly enough to commit to it, at that very moment opportunity gives birth to reality. Keep in mind that your desire to succeed carries more weight than all the stumbling blocks that lay in your path. Desire is the nutrients to help the seed planted in your mind to grow to fruition. When a desire reaches a certain level, you will suddenly notice that your chest seems to stick out a bit more, and then you discover a sweeping "S" on your undershirt. (Well, it seems like it, anyway.) You seem to have supernatural powers that enable you to do things you never believed you could. If you can dream it, you can redeem it!

Doors are opened for those who are willing to continue knocking. You may well be surprised though at who finally answers the door; it could be "The Big O" of Obstacles or "The Bigger O" of Opportunity. Which ever, you must be ready, willing and able to walk through the door and continue toward the fulfillment of your goal. The formula for success is simply this: "Want to + Will to = Done."

To get the best of what life has to offer requires you to give the best that you have to offer. Don't hold back; give it with both barrels a blazing. A person who desires something more than what they now have must be willing to give more than what they have given in the past. Desire is having the guts to try something that others do not have the stomach for. When your desire becomes a commitment, it will not take "No" for an answer. Focus your desire and you will hit the target every time.

"Want to + Will to = Done."

A desire without action is like a bird without wings - it will never get off the ground. I had the desire to write this book for the past 20+ years, but I never got around to doing it until now. Now, I can see the end in sight, or at least an end. It may very well not be the end I had envisioned, but it is an end that will be far beyond what I would have had if I had never made the decision to do something with my dream. The same is true for you. To stifle your desires is to stunt your growth. Grow on, get started!

Michelangelo said, *"Lord, grant that I may always desire more that I can accomplish."* I think I know what Mikey was saying, but you have to be careful in asking for something like that, because it can overwhelm you if you are not alert. My word of warning is this: *"Desire is desirable as long as it doesn't consume you."* We cannot permit our desires to overwhelm us to the point of allowing our priorities to get out of line, because if we do, we lose assets that were much more valuable that what we have gained.

Always be content with what you have, but never with what you are. However, we should never allow our contentment to prevent us from dreaming. When you stop dreaming, you start dying. In other words, do not give up on giving life all you have, but never allow the *wants* of life to get in the way of life itself.

"Always be content with what you have, but never with what you are."

Having a desire and a well-thought-out path to achieve it, offers hope. The same desire with no idea of what road to take will likely bring on despair. Making up your mind that you want something badly enough will erase many of the barriers that previously appeared. It has been said that the race is half over once you have made the decision to run. Desire is simply your heart telling your head that something's possible, and that things are going to change.

"If wants and wishes were frogs and fishes, we'd all be eating seafood tonight." Well, guess what, the buffet line is open! For any wish you have can become real if your desire is strong enough. Persistent passion produces results. Your desires will make things happen. "Where there is a will there is a way," and it is your desire that allows you to discover your way. Desires and dreams are what make life worth living.

Understand that detours are not dead ends but simply other ways of reaching your destiny. Be flexible in the routes you take but firm in your destination. Desire causes a thirst in people that is only quenched by the showers of success. And our desires are nothing more than our "Happy Meals" for which we hunger. Wow! With all this talk about thirst and hunger, *"You know what I'd really like?"* Promise not to tell my wife, but a Ding-Dong and a glass of chocolate milk could go a long way in bringing some satisfaction, at least for the time being.

*****

"Delight yourself in the Lord and he will give you the desires of your heart." [Psalm 37:4]

Sweet Dreams, Baby!

A great number of years ago a friend gave me a photo of a mural he had painted on his wall and it has been brought to my mind quite often since that day. I did not realize it at the time, but it is a quote by Langston Hughes. It goes like this; *"Hold fast to dreams, for if dreams die, life is but a broken winged bird that cannot fly."* I believe the truth in that statement is both profound and prophetic. It is profound in the fact that it is so simple but still so complex. Prophetic in that it predicts what will happen if we neglect our dreams. It does not say we will die if our dreams do, but the life that will be left is not my idea of what life should be. You see, birds are meant to fly, and so are we. All I can say to you is *"Sweet dreams, baby!"*

We must be very careful not to sell ourselves short when it comes to what we believe and dream. Stunting their growth will determine and hinder our level of life. Great ideas are the children of great dreams. One of the most amazing facts of life is that the best dreams happen when we go through life with our eyes wide open. The world crowns the man as "genius" who is able to hit something that others can't even see.

"Great ideas are the children of great dreams."

Do not worry about being better than someone else. Worry, if you must, about being better than you have been. Dreams generate an energy that can be found in no other source. Let them power your life! Dreams transport us to yet undiscovered worlds; shame on us, if we should fail to bring back at least one keepsake.

The mind is a manufacturing plant of thoughts, and the product we produce should always be fit for human consumption. Our dreams will be the means by which we build on our lot in life. Whether we improve the value of it or deduct from it, is up to us, and the extent to which we take action on our dreams. A life without dreams is but a skeleton of life. When you stop dreaming, you start dying!

Knowing that if the entire world were dreamers, with no doers, that nothing would ever get accomplished, never should cause us to stop dreaming. Rest assured, there will always be ample doers because of others not taking notice of their dreams. To stop dreaming may seem like a slow death, but in reality it is suicide.

"When you stop dreaming, you start dying."

To see our dreams fulfilled, we must take extra precaution in not allowing setbacks and discouragement to cause us to lose hope. There is a great deal of difference between something *knocking the breath out of us* and something that *takes our breath away;* life is one, dreams the other. Whether we see the possibility of dreams or the probability of problems will determine our course of action. To dream a dream is the easy part. To get others to believe in it as well, is the most difficult.

If what you desire is out of your reach, allow your dreams to be your ladder. It is amazing how high you can climb! When you give birth to a dream, nurture and care for it, and it will grow to make you proud.

Some are blessed with the capacity to see things that are not there, and others cursed by the same ability. To the first bunch we give the title *dreamer*, and to the second *derelict*.

Thomas Lovell Beddoes once made an interesting statement, one we should definitely entertain: *"If dreams were for sale, what would you buy?"* I believe that if we don't take the time to allow ourselves "dreaming room" we cheat not only ourselves but also the world, of what might have been. All accomplishments began life as a dream of someone.

"All accomplishments began life as a dream of someone."

May each of us, no matter how many years we have existed never allow our childlike wonder to die. The joy of dreams keeps one truly alive.

"Don't shake your head from side to side, when others see things you can't. For without the works of dreamers, our world would be quite scant!"

Dreams do not come without a price tag. However, we should not let them die simply because we cannot afford them. Others may be more than willing to invest in them. Courage and dreams must both be found in the same body. And brave indeed is the one who is willing to share his dream with others. The line of those who will tell you that it will never work stretches much farther than the one with your well-wishers.

When someone calls you a "day dreamer," thank him or her for the compliment. Those who dream with their eyes wide open are the same ones who change our world. *"Sweet dreams, baby!"*

*****

"Even though we speak like this, dear friends, we are confident of better things in your case - things that accompany salvation. God is not unjust; he will not forget your work and the love you have shown him as you have helped his people and continue to help them. We want each of you to show this same diligence to the very end, in order to make your hope sure. We do not want you to become lazy, but to imitate those who through faith and patience inherit what has been promised." [Hebrews 6:9-12]

When Good Isn't Good Enough

Satchel Paige said, *"Ain't no man that can avoid being born average, but ain't nobody got to be common."* You may not agree with his choice of words, but I do not see how you can argue with his logic. Just because a person in born into an environment that is less than desirable is not a valid reason for staying there. Each person holds within himself or herself the talent necessary to achieve excellence. Excellence does not mean that you are better than everyone else is, just better than yourself.

In striving to be the best, you can in any situation, under any circumstances, go as far as possible, and then take one more step. To strive to do things "just as well" as someone else is not an earmark of excellence. It becomes so only when it is better than the best you have ever done. When the standards you set for yourself are higher than those expected by the world, and you achieve them, at that point you have arrived at excellence- the "City of Satisfaction."

**"Each person holds within himself or herself
the talent necessary to achieve excellence."**

Even the smallest of tasks should be approached with the goal of doing them better than you did the time before. If you continue to improve in small increments, you will eventually find yourself on the doorstep of excellence, and sooner than later being invited in to stay awhile. Paying attention to, and taking action on, the small things that others do not want to do, or things they deem unimportant, will allow you to experience excellence and the rewards it has to offer. Do your best to make excellence a way of life in all you do. Anything less is not worthy of your signature.

The combination needed for excellence is to improve on what you do, and then do more of it! Never be satisfied until you know beyond any doubt that you did your best. Then and only then can you call it excellence.

It is easy to allow sloppiness to enter the picture if we, for one moment, lose sight of the finished product for which excellence is the vision. Many times we get to the point of wanting to finish a project, or grow tired of it, so that we are willing to settle for less than our best. If you are wise enough to identify sloppiness, then I trust you are wise enough to fix it.

The distance between OK and excellence is sometimes just a short step; at other times, it is a giant leap. To settle for anything other than your personal best is a disservice to society, and a disaster for you. Each new level of excellence you achieve should be the starting point for future endeavors.

Greatness means that someone was brave enough and persistent enough to attempt something that others were afraid to tackle. Excellence is made attainable by busting through walls, first in the mind and then in the world. The "ordinary" became the "extraordinary" when someone had the nerve to ignore the **stop** signs.

"…every person is your superior in at least one facet."

We fail when we allow ourselves and others to turn in work that is less than the best. The areas of excellence most easily achieved are those that match your talents. One word of warning in regard to achieving excellence: never, under any circumstances, allow yourself to think that you are better than someone else. For it is a fact that every person is your superior in at least one facet. Moreover, you can never build yourself up by tearing another down.

It seems to be a human instinct to want to do greater things, have more excitement, and leave a broader mark on the world than those who came before us. Pity the man who settles for less!

*****

"Finally, brothers, whatever is true, whatever is noble, whatever is right, whatever is pure, whatever is lovely, whatever is admirable - if anything is excellent or praiseworthy - think about such things." [Philippians 4:8]

I'll See It When I Believe It!

We often say we will believe something when we see it, but in regard to faith, I think I am closer to being right when I say, *"I'll see it when I believe it!"* I believe that anything that is worth striving for is worth visualizing and having the faith that it will come true. However, this subject of faith is not the easiest thing to write about because it is something that you are not able to touch and put your hands on. We can see the effects of it, but sometimes that just is not enough to satisfy our appetite. We may not be able to see the wind, but the effects of it are easily spotted. And we know that the sun is shining somewhere when we look up and see the moon. Looking at man, we know the Son is reflecting off him, and it gives us assurance of a brighter tomorrow. So how can we know that something exists when we haven't seen it? The answer is by faith, and a trust that the faith is true.

Faith is supported by reason, and therefore it is above reason. Reason alone does not give an accurate picture of what is true; it must be teamed with faith. Faith doesn't mean you believe something without proof; it means you have no reservations about trusting. The evidence for trusting is all around us if we will just open our eyes to it and be willing to recognize it for what it is. Faith is not blind, but in a sense it is a "seeing eye dog." It can lead us to things we would have never discovered on our own.

**"Faith is supported by reason,
and therefore it is above reason."**

If I accept only what I understand and build my world on that, my world is much too small indeed. If a man knows only what he fully understands, he understands nothing. If we believe that we must understand before we can believe, we have it reversed. No one but a fool would question the existence of the book he holds in his hand, just because he can't see the author. Faith is the art of seeing the invisible.

Saint Augustine said, *"Faith is to believe what we do not see; and the reward of this faith is to see what we believe."* Faith fuels belief and the belief fuels the being.

Some of the most important things to be seen are not visible to the eye but only come into view by way of the heart. Just because we cannot see something is no proof that it doesn't exist. Reason will only allow us to go so far. Faith opens up the way to who knows where. Faith is believing, not knowing! If we only accepted what was logical, we would not be a very accepting bunch.

"Just because we cannot see something is no proof that it doesn't exist."

We limit our faith by limiting what we believe and by what we are willing to risk and act upon. When our faith seems weak, we must remember that without it, we are lost. To live by faith is to not allow reason and proof to step foot on your land.

Our faith is affected by our thoughts. If we think little thoughts, our faith will be small. If we think big thoughts, our faith will grow large. Faith that has established limits to what it will believe is at best a dwarfed faith, and some would argue that it is no faith at all. If you want your fears to grow weaker, feed your faith! When faith has the courage to answer the door at which fear is knocking, it will find no one there. Fear and faith can never be roommates because they cannot both exist at the same time.

Faith enables us to be daring enough to try something even when we realize what could happen if we fail. If we have faith that can move mountains, we need to be willing to pick up a shovel and do our part. A German proverb goes like this: *"Begin to weave and God will provide the thread."* For our faith to become strong and remain that way, we must be willing to exercise it. For a faith to hang on when hope lets go, it must be firmly rooted and ready to stand tall in opposition to the wind.

We must have faith and believe that our lives are making a difference, or else we become confused and complacent. Faith plays a vital part in building lasting relationships. However, if you hope to be faithful to others, you first must be faithful to yourself.

Oliver Wendall Holmes once said, *"It's faith in something and enthusiasm about something that makes life worth looking at."* Faith without conviction is but a counterfeit faith. A lack of faith will keep you from enjoying the good things of this life, and the one that is to come. Faith is the proud parent of blessings.

"Faith without conviction is but a counterfeit faith."

To want more of the things we see can easily become greed; to want more of the things unseen is to desire a stronger faith. It is true that not everything can be explained. That is where faith plays its part. Faith sees the invisible, believes the incredible, and receives the impossible. So go ahead and say it with me, *"I'll see it when I believe it!"*

*****

"Now faith is being sure of what we hope for and certain of what we do not see. This is what the ancients were commended for. By faith we understand that the universe was formed at God's command, so that what is seen was not made out of what was visible." [Hebrews 11:1-3]

Freedom Is Not Free!

⌣∴∽

We live in a country that takes pride in the fact that we are free. The thing that many of us forget is the high price that others have paid for us to enjoy this extravagance, and what our obligations are to ensure its existence.

Harry S. Truman once said, *"Freedom is still expensive. It still costs money. It still costs blood. It still calls for courage and endurance. Not only in soldiers, but in every man and woman who is free and who is determined to remain free."*

Every freedom carries a certain amount of responsibility with it. If we expect to eat its fruit, we must be willing to do some work to earn it. With the word "freedom" having "free" as its root, one would naturally think they are synonymous, but they are not. Freedom means being willing to sacrifice for whatever it is you want, and free means coming without cost. Some will say that freedom of choice is the only freedom that is actually free. However, the consequences that come with it are usually very costly. Therefore, I think you would agree, *"Freedom is not free!"*

"We are all servants to something;
freedom simply gives us a choice."

In deciding what any particular freedom actually costs, we must not forget to figure in what the sacrifices we will have to make are worth to us. For everything that is gained, something else is lost. Everything worth having comes with a cost, and freedom is no exception. It is each person's responsibility to weigh the price one must pay for each chosen freedom, before the choice is made. One of the most important things we must remember in regards to freedom is that it does not mean doing whatever we please; it's having the right to do what we should.

It seems ironic but freedom simply allows us to escape from the things we do not like, to become "prisoners" of the things we enjoy. We are all servants to something; freedom simply gives us a choice. Freedom offers us the opportunity to live as we wish we could, but courage will be required to proceed.

A person's mind cannot be taken hostage without their consent, for both freedom and slavery are "mind games." Anyone who waits for someone to come and release them will forever remain a slave. We have the freedom of choice; we just need to exercise it so that it will remain healthy.

No freedom offers release until we accept it. However, many times our mind will keep us locked up behind imaginary bars that are just as tough to break free from as an actual jail cell. Many people wish for a freedom they already possess. All that needs to be done is claim it as one's own.

It's far, far better to fight for a freedom without a chance of winning than to give up freely to live as slaves. Not to choose the path of surrender means you must be willing to pay the price for the freedom you desire. Sometimes death offers a freedom from prisons from which there is no other way out. The fight for freedom may get ugly, but the benefits are beautiful.

"No freedom offers release until we accept it."

We must not allow selfish actions of others scare us to the point of not standing up and fighting for what we know is right. When a person gives in to what they know to be wrong, they become a slave to stupidity.

We must remember that if we are willing to fight for freedom, then we must be willing to extend its privileges to everyone, whether we think they are deserving or not. For one who is not willing to offer freedom to others is not worthy to enjoy it themselves.

Everyone wishes for freedom from outside restraints, but wishes the restraints to be enforced only in the actions of others. Sorry, it doesn't work that way.

A newfound freedom is in itself a rebirth, a chance to begin again. Freedom offers a chance to make decisions in regard to one's personal development, and the molding of one's character. However, sometimes we are wise enough to realize that the consequences of freedom are not worth the security our current bondage offers. For, freedom can be a frightening thing if we don't know what responsibility it brings with it. Moreover, many times after escaping from what we considered a prison, we come to the realization that it was actually a luxurious resort in comparison to our new surroundings. Freedom doesn't always come with the level of happiness we had anticipated.

One of the freedoms we hear most about is that of the freedom of speech. For me to enjoy the freedom of speech, I must realize that someone else is being forced to be a prisoner of silence. Therefore, I must be willing to trade places with them on a regular basis. The freedom of speech carries limitations with it, along with the liberties. We also must be aware of the fact that the freedom of speech means we also have the freedom to remain silent. After all, silence can sometimes speak louder than any words, right? My freedom ends where your nose begins, because none of us is free to do as we wish but just to do as we ought.

"My freedom ends where your nose begins."

One of the grandest duties we have as parents is to instill the high cost of freedom into our children. Close on the tail of that is the higher cost still of slavery. The freedoms of today are the spoils of yesterday's battles. Freedom means not having to do the things that you don't want to do. To ensure freedom for future generations, we must first convince them that it is worth fighting for, and get them to understand that without freedom, nothing else is worth having. To deserve freedom, we must be willing to do whatever it takes to keep it alive and well. *"Freedom is not free!"*

*****

"Were you not a slave when you were called? Don't let it trouble you - although if you can gain your freedom, do so."
[1 Corinthians 7:21]

"Well That's Mighty Big Of Ya!"

I have found it easier to wish for generosity in the lives of those with whom I come into contact, than to wish it so for my own life. I fear I am not that much different from any of the rest of you either. Many people try to console their conscience in regard to giving by handing out free advice. All I can say in situations like that is, *"Well that's mighty big of ya!"* True generosity gives more than advice.

In case you hadn't noticed, the one who is willing to give freely is the one who reaps the largest crop. Wisdom teaches us that the more we give the more we have. Your willingness to give and share are true signs of whether your heart is filled with love or selfishness. A love-filled heart encourages an open hand, not a closed fist. It may be possible to be generous without being loving, but it's impossible to be loving without being generous. Generosity is bred when we practice self-sacrifice. I believe that generosity is a lesson that must be taught and learned, as our natural inclination is to think only of fulfilling self.

A love-filled heart encourages an open hand, not a closed fist.

The generous person enriches his life by giving, while the one who hoards makes himself the poorest of the poor. It has been said that the truly generous person opens his pockets more and his mouth less. I believe that if we give to a cause and then spread the news to make ourselves look good, that is the only reward we will receive - if you can call that a reward. Broadcasting our generous acts will assuredly lower our credit rating with others. There are no two ways about it: generosity loses its effectiveness when its owner boasts about it.

It has been stated that more pleasure comes from giving than from lending, and when it's all said and done, the overall cost is about the same. From personal experience, I can tell you there is a lot of truth to that. I never loan money to someone with the expectation of getting it back. So, if and when I do get repaid, I am pleasantly surprised.

I owe a heartfelt "Thanks" to my wife, Linda, for teaching me to be more generous. I admit, in our early years of marriage I was not a generous individual. Some people who know me today may still think I'm stingy, but to those who think that, I can only say, "I've come a long way, baby!" I'm quick to admit that I still have a long way to go, but I am making progress. Linda already had a grip on the fact that everything we have belongs to God, and that we are mere stewards or care-takers of what has been entrusted to us. She was right: God owns it all!

Give 'till it feels good!

One of the problems with the adage of giving until it hurts is that most people have such a low tolerance of pain. J. Oswald Sanders once said, "The basic question is not how much of our money should we give to God, but how much of God's money we should keep for ourselves?"

I have read statistics that say if everyone who claims to be a Christian would simply tithe (10%), all church debt would disappear almost immediately and then the church could get down to doing God's business, mainly that of saving souls. It is a fact that we Christians need to give God what is right, instead of what is left. If you don't like the advice of "Give 'til it hurts!", then try this one; "Give 'til it feels good!"

When it comes to giving, we should take a longer look at what we have left, and a shorter one at what we have given, as it will help us to gain a truer perspective of our generosity. It is easy, if we are not careful, to give God the *credit* and keep the *cash* for ourselves. I can assure you that our society does not honor a person for what he receives, but by what he gives.

When I think of generous individuals my thoughts turn to a couple whom I have known for some 15 years or so. They both came from humble beginnings and struggled for years. The Lord then blessed them, and they in turn have blessed countless lives by their generosity. I will never forget the night the husband wrote me a check for $50,000 to help our church through a financial struggle. I know this was not the first time they have done this. This couple truly has a handle on the art of being generous.

Legend has it that a man was wandering through the desert when he happened upon a spring of cool, crystal-clear water. The water was the best he had ever tasted, and therefore he wanted to share the goodness with his king. After quenching his thirst, he quickly filled his leather canteen and began the long trek through the desert to the palace.

When he finally reached the king's court, the water had become stale because of the old leather container in which he had carried it. The king, however, graciously accepted the gift from his loyal subject, and, upon tasting it, expressed his gratitude for the gift. The wanderer went about his way with a heart filled with joy.

After the man had left, others in the king's court tasted the rank water and asked the king why he had pretended to enjoy it so much. "Oh, my dear subjects, it was not the water I tasted, but the spirit of generosity with which it was given."

Let us always remember that only a generous life is a fulfilled life, and then do all we can to make sure our life is full.

To be generous includes giving a portion of ourselves. Be generous with your money, time and encouraging words, because each of these can be life-changing to one in need. If you can learn to be generous in your giving and forgiving, your life will be blessed beyond belief.

To be generous includes giving a portion of ourselves.

All of us probably have some keepsake that we would dread the thought of having to give up. But we need to realize that if we own something that we cannot give away, it actually owns us.

Giving is just as much an act of worship as singing or praying, and is usually a better indicator of the condition of your heart. So the next time you have the opportunity to share, do it with love and a generous spirit, and you may hear someone say, *"Well that's mighty big of ya!"* and mean it!

*****

Remember this: Whoever sows sparingly will also reap sparingly, and whoever sows generously will also reap generously.
[2 Corinthians 9:6]

Goal For It!

Have you ever looked at the life of someone else and asked, "How did they get so lucky?" Most of the time if we truly checked it out, we would find that they were "lucky" because of all the preparation and hard work they exerted toward a dream or a goal they had set for themselves. It's funny how things like that "just happen!"

Wants remain wishes until you make them a goal. Then they can become reality. A person needs to have something to look forward to, or hope for, to continue progressing with this journey called life. Because when you do not, digression takes over. A goal gives a reason to get out of bed in the morning, and it's something to dream about when you lay down at night. A goal can, and will, make your life more memorable and rewarding.

To arrive successfully you must first know where you want to go. For I am sure you will agree that there is a tremendous difference between going for a walk just to get exercise, and going for a walk to end up at a specific location. Both include walking, but one has a much more defined purpose. The direction in which you are headed will determine your destination.

"Wants remain wishes until you make them a goal."

As with a newborn, once you give birth to a goal, you must take care of it. You must feed it daily and be willing to make the necessary changes (again like the newborn) to prevent it from starting to stink up your thinking process. However, you can nurture it, and be proud as you watch it grow to maturity.

Goals that are steeped in reality can turn the impossible into the probable, and the probable into certainty. Some people will falsely tell you that if your goal is defined clearly enough, you can make anything happen. I caution you that it must remain within the walls of reality. The good news is that "reality" is being redefined every day.

The weakest man with a defined goal and the determination to follow through with it is more powerful than any Goliath without a goal. When a reason for living (goal) takes hold of one's life, a newfound source of energy takes hold as well. A person with purpose will many times find obstacles moving out of their way, and, if not, they still have the power needed to go around them. If you have nowhere in particular you want to go, it does not matter what road you travel.

Reaching a goal should never be seen as a stoplight but a green light that allows you to move forward toward another one on up the road. Do not fall for the lie, "The higher you go, the easier it gets!" The reality is that the air gets thinner and the incline probably gets steeper. However, the view from the top is worth it!

Your thoughts are the driving force in your life. Either you harness them, or they will harness you. You have the power and the God-given right to sow new seeds of vision in your life today, and then enjoy the fruit for seasons to come. Just as a road map will help you to find the shortest route to a destination, so will a goal help keep you on track to your dream. One thing true of any worthwhile goal is that it must have the capacity to take you to places that you have never been before. If not, it doesn't fall under the definition of "goal."

"Your thoughts are the driving force in your life."

To aim at a goal and miss it is much more admirable that to aim at nothing and hit it. Ask yourself, "When you miss the bull's eye, was it the fault of the target, or are you to blame?"

We would not think of getting into a wagon that was hitched to a team of horses and then letting the horses decide which way to go. They will surely lead you to what most pleases them. It is the same principle with this carriage we are in called life. It will take you somewhere, but the majority of times it will be somewhere besides the place you had hoped to end up. A goal is the wheel that will permit you to steer and make necessary turns to end up at your desired destination. Having a written goal gives you the insight to say, "Gittee Up!"

If you find yourself born into poverty, take no blame. If you find yourself staying there, accept the shame. In the end, our life is very much like a book, of which we write a page each day. Each of us must ask ourselves, "Will mine be worth reading?"

I know some people who seem to be perfectly content to drive a vehicle at 25 miles an hour, ever knowing that the speedometer is registered up to 160. If you are happy with that, then so be it. However, for the rest of us who want to appreciate the thrill of maximum performance on a fast track or interstate highway, we ask that you stay in the slow lane, and out of our way, because we are "goaling" for it!

*****

"This is a trustworthy saying. And I want you to stress these things, so that those who have trusted in God may be careful to devote themselves to doing what is good. These things are excellent and profitable for everyone." [Titus 3:8]

Habits Are Habit Forming!

ꌤ

I read a story one time about a man who flew his own plane but grew tired of having to drive from the airport to his cabin on the lake. So he decided to put pontoons on his plane so that he could just land on the lake and walk to the cabin.

However, it seems that on his first trip after having the plane converted, he prepared to land at the airport as he always had in the past. His wife was with him, and she realized what was about to happen and screamed just in time for him to pull the plane back up.

He said very little on the ride to the lake, but after making a safe arrival, he heaved a sigh of relief and told his wife, "That was one of the dumbest things I have ever done!" Then he proceeded to open the door to the plane, stepped out and fell directly into the… lake!

What can I say? Old habits die hard. Let's face it: the mind has a terrible time forgetting what we have told it for forever to be the truth. If we continually do something for long enough, it gets to the point where we do it without thinking.

Horace Mann made the comment, *"Habits are like a cable. We weave a strand of it everyday and soon it cannot be broken."* I am pretty sure that was his way of saying, *"Habits are habit forming!"*

"Habits will become either stronger or weaker on a daily basis, depending on what we feed them."

A habit does not become a habit overnight and neither can we lose it quickly. Habits begin their lives in such weak condition that we don't think they have a chance for survival. However, before we realize it, they have become so powerful that we have a tough time getting them under control. Habits will become either stronger or weaker on a daily basis, depending on what we feed them. If we are trying to replace a bad habit with a good one, the bad one will be stronger at the start, but will grow weaker due to starvation. The good one will be weaker at the start and continue to grow stronger from the daily nourishment and practice. We must first get control of our habits in our minds, and then we move on to controlling them in our actions.

In attempting to make or break a habit, we must make every effort possible to not miss a single day of action in that regard. For if we do, we fall farther behind schedule than we were on the day of omission. In the early stages of developing a habit, we are in control, but soon the roles are reversed. It is a fact that the easier it is to do something, the harder it is to stop.

"We must accept responsibility for every habit that lives in us."

Sometimes one of the most important steps in breaking a bad habit is to change the people you hang around with, and the places you had frequented when you acquired the habit in the first place. If bad habits did not bring such tremendous levels of satisfaction with them, it would not be nearly so difficult to do away with them.

The good news is that if our intention is strong enough and we are persistent enough, we can and will overcome any bad habit. Mark Twain said, *"Habit is habit, and not to be flung out of the window by any man, but coaxed downstairs a step at a time."* The best advice in dealing with bad habits is not to allow them to start in the first place.

Odd, isn't it, how we are blinded to our own downfalls, but have 20/20 vision when looking at our neighbors. It is a person's habits that make them different from another. We are all created equal, but we pick up habits that make us who we are. We must accept responsibility for every habit that we have. Oh, we can play the blame game and point a finger at anyone we want to, but we still own them.

We must know that we alone are responsible for the role we allow them to play in our daily lives.

It is certain that if we realized what a tremendous part habits play in our lives, we would be more careful in deciding which ones we allow to take up residence. It has been estimated that 90% of our everyday lives are the result of the habits we have adopted. Our thoughts soon turn to action, our actions become habits, and our habits define who we are.

Is it just me, or does it seem that good habits are easier to give up than bad ones? It just doesn't seem fair, does it?

The more often we do something, the more likely we will do it yet again, and we will become what we repeatedly do. Habits never become habit all at once, but little by little. If we can prevent a habit from showing up at practice time, we can keep him out of the game. Practice is what makes a habit develop. If we continually give into our habits, it won't be long until they convince us that they are a necessity, and that is when they are so hard to give up. It's like I said in the beginning, *"Habits are habit forming!"*

*****

"No temptation has seized you except what is common to man. And God is faithful; he will not let you be tempted beyond what you can bear. But when you are tempted, he will also provide a way out so that you can stand up under it." [1 Corinthians 10:13]

Well, To Be Honest With You

I appreciate the story of Babe Didrikson Zaharias, the late golf champion, and how one time she disqualified herself from a gold tournament for having hit the wrong ball out of the rough. Speaking with a friend after this incident, the friend said, "But no one would have ever known about it if you had just gone on, as if nothing had happened." Babe's reply was a classic: "I would have known!" Babe knew honor is worth more than any amount of money gained through dishonest means.

"Honesty is a victory every time."

Honesty is a victory every time. Dishonesty means you lose, no matter what the scorecard reads. To lose honestly is simply to have lost only once, but to win in a dishonest manner means you lose all your life. I must admit that it is not always easy to be honest, but I still hold to the fact that it is, and always has been, the best policy in dealing with myself or others. You ask, "Have I always been honest in all my dealings?" And my answer would be, *"Well, to be honest with you..."*

Each of us is faced with two paths, and we must choose one. Either the path of dishonesty, that is chosen by the "near sighted" who can't see the danger that lies ahead, or the path of honesty that holds the best of what the world has to offer. In making your choice, you decide your destiny. Ask yourself, "Does the path I'm on benefit others as well as myself?" If so, stick with it. If not, abandon it immediately!

In choosing between right and wrong, it doesn't seem fair, but the wrong way often seems the easy way, while the right way takes a bit more effort. Therefore, if the road you are on seems to be smooth and flat, be cautious, and take the next exit on the "right" side to get back on track. For an honest person, taking the path of least resistance is usually not the best path.

Things of the world pale when compared to the things of character. Wealth and beauty are fragile and only last for a short while, but the worth and beauty of honesty increases as time goes by. Being honest means being able to live with yourself without regrets. Right and wrong are opponents who have been doing their best to defeat the other since the beginning of time. The question each of us must answer is, "Whose corner are you in?"

"Being honest means being able to live with yourself without regrets."

To make yourself into an honest person is to guarantee the world of one less menace to society. To dress your words in robes of honesty will make them appropriately dressed, no matter what the occasion or style. Honesty is the best policy, but the world sure could use a few more policyholders!

A dentist was overheard telling his patient, just as he was about to insert a hypodermic needle into his mouth, "Now you may feel just a little stick when I put this needle in. On the other hand, it might feel like you are getting kicked in the mouth by a mule!" I guess you might as well tell it like it is, if you are going to tell it. For you see, honesty is a big deal even in the little things.

When a person emphasizes how honest they are, it's probably not the first lie they have ever told. It is silly to believe that everyone you meet is going to treat you in an honest manner, but sillier still to think that none will. If you must err, do so on the side of believing everyone to be honest - at least until he or she has had the chance to prove otherwise. Honesty becomes a more sought- after commodity when a person realizes just how harmful dishonesty is. None of us likes to hear things that point out the flaws in our character, but a true friend is not one who tells us just what we like to hear. A true friend is honest with us, and offers kind, gentle suggestions on how we might improve. If you resolve to keep only company with honest characters, be assured of a small crowd; however, you'll know that you won't be taken advantage of.

Honesty is not measured by degrees; you either have it or you don't. When you are dishonest to someone else, you are first dishonest with yourself. Honesty is not only the best policy, but if it is strictly adhered to, no other policies are needed. There is no other character trait that plays a greater role in determining the success of a person than honesty. You need to invest everything you possibly can in honesty, for it pays double dividends, both in peace of mind and in financial gain.

**"Honesty is not measured by degrees;
You either have it or you don't."**

Some folks can only handle a little truth at a time, but if they are silly enough to ask for more, let them have it! It may very well be what they need to keep them from making the mistake of a lifetime. Truth is made out of tough stuff. You can kick it around all day and it is in just as good a shape at the end as it was at the start.

No matter how long we try to avoid it, eventually each of us will be forced to face the consequences of our actions. Good acts meet with good consequences, and vise-versa. The good are rewarded while the bad are punished.

It is true that a person's character is worth a fortune, so be careful how you spend yours. The fruits of right living bring nourishment to the soul, and it provides the orchard for the benefit of future generations. If we are to know the quality of a person's honesty and sincerity, they must constantly be handing out samples. We must continually ask ourselves whether the samples we are giving out would make people want to come back and get some of what we have, or would it be thrown into the trash barrel as useless? *"Well, to be honest with you..."*

*****

"Do not repay anyone evil for evil. Be careful to do what is right in the eyes of everybody." [Romans 12:17]

Humble Pie

I am not sure what all the ingredients are for "humble pie" recipe, but I am sure that crow is the main one. Moreover, it does not seem to make a difference what you choose to drink with it because it just does not lie well on the stomach. If we could learn the lesson of humility, it would leave more room in our system for other more palatable items.

A preacher visited a convenience store and picked up a dollar pack of mints but soon discovered that he had forgotten to bring any money with him. Not wanting to leave without his mints, he jokingly said to the cashier, "I would be glad to invite you to hear me preach, but I don't have any dollar sermons." The cashier never missed a beat with her reply, "Perhaps I could come twice." I am sure he got the message!

"As soon as you think you have humility, you do not!"

The fact that the size of the crowd at your funeral will be determined, at least to some degree, by the weather conditions should help keep your head from swelling.

True humility has more drawing power than the most powerful of magnets; false humility is a sure repellant. St. Bernard said, *"It is no great thing to be humble when you are brought low; but to be humble when you are praised is a great and rare attainment."*

Humility is the ability to be just as comfortable in the back row as you would be in the front.

When you are announced as the victor, and inside you are leading the applause, pride is the only real winner. As soon as you are sure you have humility, you do not!

Comparing ourselves to someone else can instill a false humility. The truth is revealed when we compare ourselves with the only perfect person to ever live - Jesus Christ. It doesn't take long to realize just how far from the mark we really are.

Harold C. Chase's quote in regards to humility really sums it up well. He said, *"The wise person possesses humility. He knows that his small island of knowledge is surrounded by a vast sea of the unknown."* Even the most learned person knows only a small percentage of the knowledge that exists in the world. Just knowing that should help us keep our perspective in line.

If our words are used to sing "self praise." we will always be off- key. Humility is well displayed when someone who is talented enough to play first violin agrees to play "second fiddle" and thinks nothing of it.

As sure as the mouse scurries from the cat, so does humility when pride is the predator.

Humility is a cornerstone on which all Christian character should be built.

It is true that the one who thinks himself big appears small to others. When humility is in proper working order, we will think of ourselves less and more of others. However, one of the most difficult things to do is not feel good when your opponent suffers defeat. True humility is to see yourself as God sees you. By the way, He does look at things differently than we do.

True humility is to see yourself as God sees you.

How would you answer if you found yourself in front of the Pearly Gates awaiting admission into heaven along with one other person, and St. Peter appeared and said, "We've got room for only one more. Which one of you is more humble?"

*****

"Do nothing out of selfish ambition or vain conceit, but in humility consider others better than yourselves." [Philippians 2:3]

I Just Can't Imagine

How long has it been since you let your imagination run wild? Where did it take you? Oh, I can only imagine! My next is question is, "Why don't you do it more often?" Now you may be thinking that it is none of my business, and you would be exactly right. However, it is *your* business!

I have no doubt that you can remember having what some might call a "vivid" imagination or a "wild" imagination when you were younger. However, I am almost afraid that with all of the video games and television that children play and watch today, they just do not exercise their imagination muscles as much as we used to, or as much as they should. Our imagination, if we will allow it to, will take us to places we can only well imagine. To limit your imagination is to limit your life.

Do not allow your imagination to deny you the beauty the world has to offer. Allow your imagination to explore on its own - you will be amazed at the golden nuggets it uncovers. *"I just can't imagine"* what all of those treasures will be, but I look forward to hearing about them as you let your imagination run wild.

**"Do not allow your imagination to deny you of the beauty
the world has to offer."**

Before anything can become a reality it has to earn its wings in the Institute of Imagination. What is real is limited, but what is imaginary is unlimited. Jump-start your imagination with the charge to "Lead on!"

Another positive thing about our imagination is that through it we can foresee possible issues that could be a danger, and possibly make the necessary changes to avert them. We need to allow our imaginations to visualize what it is you are dreaming of, and this will enable your subconscious mind to begin the work for you. Our imagination is not limited by walls, ceiling or floor, but is allowed to live wherever it chooses. Let it run free.

Be careful not to limit your imagination, for this is where miracles begin. Knowledge without an imagination to go with it is but an idle bag of ideas. Gather all the information you can, ponder it repeatedly, and then turn your imagination loose and let it run. Many times, we allow our imaginations to grow lazy, and thus prevent us from ever knowing the joy of living life to its fullest. Your imagination is your servant, so take full advantage of it!

"Your imagination is your servant, so take full advantage of it!"

Your imagination will stretch your mind to such an extent that it will never return to its original shape. You have heard of people having "warped" minds, haven't you? Well, I am sorry to tell you, but that was not from their imagination going crazy, but was probably the result of a severe blow to the head from sometime in their past life. However, if you want to blame it on the imagination going bananas help yourself.

The best indicator we have for what is in store for the future is our imagination because that is where dreams are made. Our imagination is a time machine that can take us back in time or into the future, both in the same day. Our imagination of today will allow us to travel to worlds that did not exist yesterday. Imagination teamed with insight discovers a completely new world. Limiting your imagination is limiting what could be.

"Limiting your imagination is limiting what could be."

We must understand that the seeds that will give birth to the future lie dormant in the mind of humanity, just waiting for someone to awaken them. Never allow the way things are to limit the greatness of how things could be.

Imagination is not the possession of only the "rich and famous" - all have unlimited access, if they wish. Your imagination gives you visiting rights to the ideas of others and allows the opportunity to gain insight and see things as they do. What a blessing! When we do this, our imagination is an instrument of peace, for it allows us to walk a mile in another's shoes.

On the other hand, your imagination can play tricks on you, so stay alert and realize the magic has just begun. Our imagination is the laboratory of the mind where possibilities are examined and discoveries are made. To see possible solutions to the problem at hand, allow your imagination to take you all the way around it and therefore see it from different angles. Imagination holds the light for possibility as it makes its way to the house of reality. You might notice that there are no "off limit" signs posted in the lawns of your imagination, so give it free reign. The most efficient proving ground for any of our ideas is on the Isle of Imagination.

**"Never allow the way things are
to limit the greatness of how things could be."**

Let your imagination take pictures of what you dream of, and then proceed with the developing process. The imagination is the manufacturing plant for possibilities; make sure yours is open for business.

Understand that everything had its beginning in the mind of someone. Imagination is the creator of opportunity, and the endless world of the heart. Never grow so old that you allow the facts to dim the vision of your imagination. Imagination opens our eyes to the opportunities around us. The way I look at it, imagination should receive the "Entertainer of the Year" award, for its ability to enthrall its audience.

If you wish your life to have happiness, imagine it so, and it will be. For your imagination is an unopened treasure chest, filled with golden dreams and beset with jewels of possibilities. So go ahead, try it on for size. *"I just can't imagine"* anything looking better than you do, dressed in the finest that the world has to offer.

*****

"And this is my prayer: that your love may abound more and more in knowledge and depth of insight, so that you may be able to discern what is best and may be pure and blameless until the day of Christ, filled with the fruit of righteousness that comes through Jesus Christ - to the glory and praise of God." [Philippians 1:9-11]

My Kind of Kindness.

I can't remember who gets the credit for starting the "random acts of kindness" movement a number of years ago, but I only wish it had been me. But since it wasn't, I can still do my share by doing what it suggests, - looking for ways on a daily basis to be kind to others just for the sake of being kind; not doing it for selfish reasons, but because it is the right thing to do. I really do believe the world- and everyone in it- would be better off if we adopted this kind of behavior, rather than let our selfishness rule our everyday life. I guarantee you that each of us could be kinder than we are.

Kindness is the thread that sews souls together.

Have you ever noticed that the unkind are exactly those who need kindness? However, in dealing with unkind people, if we can be kinder than the moment deserves, we can have hours of cooperation and a lifetime of joy. If you don't wait until tomorrow to treat people with kindness and understanding, today will be a better day for both of you. To make the sun shine brighter tomorrow, radiate kindness today.

Kindness is the thread that sews souls together. And one of the neat things about kindness is this: kindness makes both the giver **and** the receiver feel better about themselves. A kind word can pick me up when trouble has knocked me down, and it can do the same for anyone you extend it to. Kindness is like 10W-30; it's the lubricant that oils relationships and allows them to run smoothly. I am sure that is the reason why our most meaningful relationships are always laced with kindness.

A number of years ago Linda and I traveled to Australia to celebrate our 25th anniversary. One of the things we tried to do there was throw a boomerang, to see if we could get it to come back to us. The joy of success in doing so reminds me that when I take the time to throw out kindness, it will return to me. The surest way of receiving kindness is by giving it to others first. Kind words are music to our ears and make us sing from the heart.

Kindness warms the coolest heart.

It seems that we live in a world where selfishness often guides our thoughts and actions. When we do this, kindness is stifled because we are concerned more about what we are going to get than what we are capable of giving. To add value to any day, show kindness to others without regard to what your reward might be. Kindness is contagious; spreading it to others will make a sick soul well. Kindness warms the coolest heart.

I can't begin to tell you how many people I have heard complain about not having any friends. I believe one of the reasons for that is because they are quick to point out the shortcomings of others, and in so doing become blind to their own imperfections. I have found that people who are good at overlooking slights they incur from others, and are willing to look for ways to show acts of kindness to those around them, will have little or no problem in maintaining friendships. Don't take my word for it. Try it, and see if I am not right. You have little to lose and a new world of friends to gain.

When you think about it, to think an unkind thought of another and not share it, is in itself an act of kindness. I won't argue for a minute that it would have been kinder still to not have thought the unkind thing in the first place, but sometimes our "thinker" gets ahead of our heart. Think about this: the meaning of the word kindness is to love someone more than they deserve. The other person may have deserved to hear the unkind thought your thinker had processed, but applying the definition of kindness allowed you to keep your thoughts hidden.

A small seed of kindness shown to another can grow into a bumper crop of confidence and hope. Therefore, we should all sow kindness abundantly.

Kind actions are fueled by kind thoughts.

Kind words are good, but, when accompanied by action, the end result is far better than good - it is great! Kind actions are fueled by kind thoughts. We cannot have kind thoughts of others when we are absorbed with selfishness. Once again we must be willing to lay aside our wants and desires to be the kind person we should be. You would be hard-pressed to argue against the fact that kindness betters everything it touches, and it pays great dividends when invested in others.

Single drops of kindness can erode a heart of stone. Kindness can break down walls that have withstood the forces of hatred and misunderstanding. Be aware that the change of heart in the person you are kind to may not - and probably won't - happen quickly. However, over time you will notice that the sharpness in another's voice is not quite so harsh as it had once been. I believe that if we only knew the hurts endured by others, kindness would come more freely. And I know that when kindness goes head-to-head with hatred and anger, kindness wins every time.

We should be concerned about being kind to the adults in our everyday world, as well as to children. Kindness shown to a child will create fond memories in their heart. I can attest to this. When I was growing up, one uncle always showed me kindness and had time to talk and joke with me, even when other adults were present. This gave me a feeling of being special. I only hope I can build fond memories in the hearts of the young people with whom I come into contact.

Kindness is a language that everyone can understand.

In our travels, Linda and I have been fortunate enough to visit over forty countries. Even in countries where we couldn't under-stand a single word they spoke, we had no trouble understanding an act of kindness when it was extended. Kindness is a language that everyone can understand. Kindness is sunshine for the soul, so, go ahead; let your little light shine! Don't wait for tomorrow; do a random act of kindness today. Better yet, do one today and every tomorrow that you are blessed with on this earth. From a kind heart, love flows.

*****

"Be kind and compassionate to one another, forgiving each other, just as in Christ God forgave you." [Ephesians 4:32]

Why, That Lazy, No Good Bum!

Have you ever known someone who seemed to have so much natural ability and yet they never seemed to apply themselves to much of anything? Well, we have a name for people like that in the neck of the woods I come from…LAZY! It makes me sick when I think of what people who fall into this category throw away.

I remember watching an episode of the TV show "Hee-Haw" some 45 years ago. One of the skits was of two old hillbillies laying side-by-side on the ground resting. A pretty girl walked beside one of the fellows, and he mentioned the fact to his friend, who replied, "Boy, I wish I was lookin' that way." He was too lazy to turn his head to enjoy one of the nicer things in life! All I could say then was, *"Why that lazy, no good bum!"* and I would repeat that thought today. Laziness is king in the land of Might-Have-Been.

"The only sure way to get started is to get started!"

I am afraid that we have generated a generation that just doesn't have the get-up-and-go to apply themselves like we used to. Now don't get me wrong, I know my generation as well as all the others before them had its share of lazy people, too, but I can't help but believe that there is a greater percentage today. They seem to have the attitude that the world owes them a living, and they will just wait for somebody to deliver it to them. I don't know of an easy way to break the news to them other than this: the only sure way to get started is to get started! Laziness will prevail unless it is forced into action by the force of need. Muster the will to begin and you have the will to win.

All the journeys ever made had the same beginning; taking the first step. I have heard it said that a task is half finished the moment it begins. Logically this makes no sense, but it makes all the sense in the world when applied to reality. I am not sure why it is so hard for us to come up with a plan and then begin working toward its completion. But one thing is for sure, a job that's never started will never be finished.

Getting ready to live and truly living are two entirely different states. I have known people who have dreamed dreams but never took action on them, and therefore missed out on all the good things that might have been. The worst thing a person can do is to never try - and then spend the rest of their life wondering if they could have succeeded?

Sir Walter Scott's quote is worth repeating in regards to never getting started. He said, "To be always intending to live a new life, but never finding the time to set about it - this is as if a man should put off eating and drinking from one day to another till he is starved and destroyed." Never getting started will cause the dreams of the mightiest to starve and eventually destroy any potential there might have been.

I am sure procrastination and laziness are cousins even though I have never traced the family tree of either one. We usually refer to our own delay in getting started on a project as falling into the category of "procrastination" and reserve the term "lazy" to the other fellow's idleness. Funny how we do that, isn't it?

Laziness has a way of growing on people, and if one's not careful, it can consume the whole. The willingness to overcome inertia is the first step on the road to achieving greatness. Once again, it is that first step that proves the hardest. *"Tomorrow* is the lazy person's answer to *When?"* The biggest fool is he who thinks he will start tomorrow.

A young man from our local school corporation, when asked by the teacher to write an essay on *"The effects of laziness,"* turned in a blank sheet of paper. I can't help but wonder what sort of score he got.

Never beginning is to birth failure.

I sometimes think that little is accomplished because little is attempted. We find it easier to just sit around and wait on winning the lottery, or having a rich relative kick the bucket, than do something for ourselves. You can be motivated but take no action, but you will discover that once you act, the motivation will come. Never beginning is to birth failure. The only way a person will ever know their potential is to overcome idleness, and begin to begin. Don't be hindered by thinking you can only do a little; do the little you can! For if everyone pitched in and did their part, this world would be a much more productive place.

"I am going to wait until…" is the motto of the lazy. No matter when the thing they first named happens, they will think of something else to take its place. They live in the land of *One of These Days*! Just as a spectator never won a race, the victory goes to the one willing to run.

Once you have defined your plan to achieve your goal, get started on it at once, though you may not think you're ready. If you wait too long, you are sure to hear someone say, *"Why, that lazy, no good bum!"* and we don't need another reason not to do it!

*****

Laziness brings on deep sleep, and the shiftless man goes hungry.
[Proverbs 19:15]

Lead, Follow
Or Get Out Of The Way!

～:～

There have been world leaders who have led by force and leaders who have led by example, but the one thing they had in common was that they were able to get people united in their actions toward the fulfillment of a goal. Leadership means winning others to the team, and making them feel as if they are a vital part of any anticipated victories. You can do this by Lording your authority over those under your command, or by persuading them that we are all in it together. Leadership that scares subordinates into action does nothing to build a permanent force, for once the current threat passes, you have to get everyone back on board with yet another scare tactic. True leadership is not a lordship but a kinship of family. The ability to instill confidence in those who are following your lead is necessary for any one in a leadership capacity. If you find yourself not being able to do just that, then do not be surprised to hear somebody say, *"Lead, follow or get out of the way!"*

"True leadership is not a lordship but a kinship of family."

A leader must be willing not only to accept the full blame when anything goes wrong but also to give the praise to others when things go right. A leader looks for and develops the specific talents of those under his or her charge, and allows them to become all they can be. The leader must learn not to interfere with progress that is being made by over-supervising the situation at hand, but to allow the people to do the job before them. Leaders need to have the capacity to take their followers to places beyond where they are now, or have ever been before. The best leaders have the ability to allow others to see the presence of possibilities, and gently persuade them in that direction. All great leaders not only serve in the capacity of coach but head cheerleader as well. A leader's goal should always be centered on the betterment and development of those under his charge, and never around self-fulfillment. This being the case, rewards will result.

Sometimes the most effective way to lead is to let your followers know that you are behind them all the way. I love the way Alexander Ledru-Rollin phrased it: *"I've got to follow them, I am their leader."* The majority of dedicated leaders understand that leadership has more to do with action than position. Life has been likened to a dog sled team, in that the ones following can only go as fast as the lead dog. Make sure, if you are in a position of leadership, that you are not slowing those down who are following, but allowing them to become all they can be.

A person who has not proved himself or herself as a servant has not yet earned the right to lead. Henry Ford said this in regard to who should be the leader; *"The question 'Who ought to be the boss?" is like asking, "Who ought to be the tenor in the quartet?" Obviously it is the man who can sing tenor."* Not everyone has what it takes to be leaders, but that is OK; for if all were leaders, who would follow? A leader leads by words and deeds, and the best example is a living example. However, before a leader can be successful in leading others, he or she must be able to lead self.

"Vision is vital if a leader has hopes of tasting victory."

A leader should always share any encouragement with the troops but guard any fears as "top-secret." The true test of a leader comes when the going gets tough because when all is running smoothly things mostly take care of themselves. Vision is vital if a leader has hopes of tasting victory. However, vision alone is not sufficient; the torch must be passed onto others. Leadership is getting people to be willing to make sacrifices for the benefit of others as well as for themselves. Until those under your leadership know you care about them, they will not be willing to give their all. Leaders must have confidence and be willing and able to instill that same confidence in others. If a leader does not have hope, he is leading a hopeless bunch. If a leader cannot inspire, he cannot lead. In the same way, if a leader is not a mentor, the ship is going down!

One of the greatest military leaders of modern America was General George S. Patton, and the example in the following quote shows why that is the case. *"Now, we have the finest food, equipment, the best spirit, and the best men in the world. You know, by God, I actually pity those poor people we're going up against."* It is easy to see from this how he could give his troops the hope they so desperately needed for winning. Leaders who are able to win the respect of the followers are the same ones who produce more than they promise. I think you would have to agree that General Patton certainly fell into this category.

"If a leader does not have hope he is leading a hopeless bunch."

A leader decides what language will be spoken in the management of everyday affairs; words of encouragement and hope need to be the native tongue. A leader must use words that say, "We can." not "I will." The fundamentals must be made "fun" in the "mental" states of everyone involved, and it is up to the leader to see to it.

If an automobile is to stay on the road and between the lines, it cannot afford to allow every rider to have a steering wheel. The same is true in any leadership capacity; one person only can have control to make sure they stay en route to where they are headed.

What a sickening feeling to be in a leadership capacity and to look back over your shoulder and notice that no one is following. However, another issue some leaders struggle with is whether the ones in back are following or chasing. As leaders, we must know our instructions are clear and easy to follow. Unlike the gym teacher who told the students to *"Pair up in groups of three, and then line up in a circle."* Huh? Maybe it's time for someone to say, *"Lead, follow or get out of the way."*

*****

"Be diligent in these matters; give yourself wholly to them, so that everyone may see your progress. Watch your life and doctrine closely. Persevere in them, because if you do, you will save both yourself and your hearers." [1 Timothy 4:15-16]

True Blue

The story is told of a young private who was preparing for a fierce battle with the enemy. Before departing for his spot on the front line, he handed his buddy a letter and said, *"If I happen not to make it back and you do, please see that this letter gets delivered to Ruth. Tell her my last thoughts were of her, and her name was the last words I spoke. Here's another letter for Susie as well. Tell her the same thing."*

Now I don't know about you, but I think this young man had the wrong idea about the meaning of loyalty. For you see, one of the greatest virtues we can hope to possess is dependability. When we are dependable and loyal, we are what one might call *true blue.*

If there is one key that opens the locks on getting a job and keeping it, it is loyalty. However, I might add that loyalty seems to be a rare commodity in today's world. Being in sales for the past 35 years, I can tell you that the loyalty level has definitely declined in most every facet of the business world. It seems now that the majority of all the decisions made are based on the lowest cost involved, and many times that ends up with a much higher price tag than before. Lack of loyalty is one pathway to failure.

"Lack of loyalty is one pathway to failure."

The real problem in most organizations is not a lack of effective leaders but a lack of loyal followers. I do believe, however, that the most effective leader and the most effective follower share the characteristic of loyalty. The loyalty of an employee is usually patterned after the loyalty of the employer. Loyalty has a trickle-down effect and touches all who happen to be standing down- stream. Many companies, institutions, nations and marriages fall because loyalty is no longer a core value. I believe the world would be a better place if all of us were more loyal in our dealings.

When your loyalty allows you to do what is right even when faced with opposition, you have won the battle, no matter what the critics say. Displaying loyalty in your life will make you appear as a fool in the eyes of many, but I challenge you to be loyal anyway. As a matter of fact, wrap that loyalty with love and kindness, and you will win the hearts of all you encounter.

We need to be so dependable and loyal to our friends that if we tell them we'll be somewhere and then not show up, they'll send flowers! Loyalty without faithfulness is but an alias. Loyalty is a combination of common decency and common sense. It means giving yourself to a cause and making that cause a vital part of who you are.

"Loyalty without faithfulness is but an alias."

It is a shame that history is filled with more stories of loyalty displayed by one's dog than by his friends, but that seems to be the case. If you notice, a dog will wag his tail and make his master feel important every time it sees him. However, many times it seems that our human "friends" are glad to see us only when they think we can benefit them in some way.

If there is one element that will cover a multitude of weaknesses it is loyalty. If you are true in all your dealings, and are loyal to those you deal with, they will have a tendency to overlook your shortcomings. Loyalty and devotion in small deeds make for a big deal. Whatever you try, give it all you've got, and remain loyal to the end. When you do, you will find others are much more likely to get behind you and support you. And when all is said and done, more will be done than said by the joint effort.

Money can buy a servant but not his loyalty. Loyalty is a heart issue, and heart issues carry no price tags. Loyalty also shows signs of being related to courage because both seem to emerge more clearly when under stress. Loyalty goes to the head of the class when virtuous living is taught.

"Loyalty and devotion in small deeds makes for a big deal."

The Bible is filled with examples of people (Joseph, Paul, David, Peter, etc.) who made loyalty an integral part of their lives and were rewarded richly. Not only were their lives made richer by loyal deeds, but the lives of those they touched were enriched as well. May we all trust that God will enrich and strengthen our lives when we make loyalty a regular commodity in our daily lives.

I have heard it said that family life teaches you loyalty, patience, understanding, perseverance, and a lot of other things you wouldn't have needed if only you'd stayed single!

There is some humor in that last statement, but I would have to disagree with the logic that goes along with it. I don't care who you are or what kind of position you hold in life, you will need loyalty, patience, understanding, perseverance and a lot of other things to make it through the day, whether you're married or single. And I believe the rewards of developing those characteristics in your character will help you become *"true blue!"* I wish for you the brightest of colors!

*****

"...keep this desire in the hearts of your people forever, and their hearts loyal to you." [1 Chronicles 29:18b]

How Lucky Can You Get?

We have all probably known someone in our lifetime that seemed to be a magnet for good luck. You have heard, and may have even used, the old saying that someone is so lucky that he could *"step into a bucket of poop and come out smelling like a rose!"*

Now, I would have to admit that a situation like that would have to involve something rather than just good karma because there is quite a difference in the aroma of the two. However, I would be hard-pressed to attribute all a person's good fortune to the thing we call "luck." It is a fact that the amount of preparation determines the amount of luck that will be present when opportunity arises. So when we ask the question, *"How lucky can you get?"* I guess before we could answer, we would have to know just how long that person has been working and preparing for the task at hand. At least, having that information would enable us to make an educated guess as to just how much luck was about to show up.

This thing called *luck* is a "sixth sense" because it seems to know when to take advantage of the opportunity at hand. Some use the name "Lucky" to describe the right person, at the right place, at the right time. It sounds to me like "Mr. Right" might be a better name for him. Few have gotten *lucky* who did not lay their foundation with tons of toil and pounds of perspiration. Luck seems to be joined at the hip with hard work, and multiple attempts to separate the two have never been successful.

The joke is told of a man who owned a hardware store and made regular deliveries to his good customers. One day on his route, he accidentally ran down an elderly woman. She sued him, and won the case for a sizable amount of cash. So large indeed, that he was forced to close up shop. However, he continued to work hard and in a few short years was able to open in a new location. As fate would have it, he had not been open for more than a few short months when he had another accident that resulted in yet another lawsuit. The same results as the first. Once more, he had to close up shop. Then one quiet Saturday afternoon he was sitting in his den reading the paper when his young son came running into the house yelling, *"Daddy, daddy. Come quick! Mom has just been hit by a semi!"* The man's eyes filled with tears. He was overcome with emotion but managed to say, *"Well, praise the Lord, my luck has finally changed!"*

That story almost makes me want to ask again, *"How lucky can you get?"* Some people seem to get bad luck and good luck confused.

Luck is the offspring of preparation and opportunity tying the knot. Sometimes we are shocked when *luck* arrives before a nine-month waiting period, and other times we have to struggle with "labor pains" for years on end before it shows up. Luck and chance are sometimes mistaken for twins, but it is not so, for luck belongs to your family, and chance, I am afraid, to mine.

"Luck is the offspring of preparation and opportunity tying the knot."

Luck seems to favor those who are willing to take action on their beliefs. Luck is the leftovers from the five-course meal of dreams, action, hard work, sweat, and persistence. An old Persian proverb says, *"Go and wake up your luck."* Luck has more to do with paying attention and being ready than it does anything else. Lucky is the man who baits his hook well! Plan well, execute well, and enjoy the spoils of luck.

If luck seems to be beating you in the bout of life, don't hold back, hit him with everything you've got and let him not soon forget that he has been to battle. Armand Hammer once remarked, *"When you work seven days a week, fourteen hours a day, you get lucky."* It is a fact that being prepared by being educated and being prone to hard work and integrity does seem to up one's chances of being lucky. Luck is an accident that trips over the idle and lands in the lap of the diligent.

Too bad our level of luck is not the same in the drawing for a sweepstakes winner as it is in being selected to serve on jury duty. Luck is a word that has different definitions, depending on who we happen to be talking about. If it is our self, luck is the result of hard work; if it is our neighbor, luck is just plain luck. Have you ever wondered why it is that Lady Luck goes steady with Willy the Worker, and Lazy Larry sits home alone? Think about it.

"Luck is an accident that trips over the idle and lands in the laps of the diligent."

It is silly to fell a tree and then leave it, thinking luck will find it and cut it up and split it and stack it on the back porch. It is not going to happen! Forget about luck. Just pull your work boots on and give it all you've got.

I think you will find as you go through life that luck sometimes comes to visit, but seldom stays for an extended period of time. Luck is usually not a mistake as it shows up where hard work and persistence reside.

Some consider a rabbit's foot to be lucky but I feel sure if you checked with the crippled rabbit he would dare to disagree. It has been proven that if you combine common sense and the Golden Rule you will not need a rabbit's foot for good luck, because the bad stuff just does not come around. Luck, whether good or bad, can be closely linked to the same type of judgment. Knowing that, how would you answer the question *"How lucky can you get?"*

*****

"He whose walk is blameless is kept safe, but he whose ways are perverse will suddenly fall." [Proverbs 28:18]

I Thought I Was Wrong Once, But I Was Mistaken!

We could look high and low trying to find a person alive who has not made a mistake in the past twenty-four hours. I truly believe the only way we could do it is to find someone who has been unconscious for the past day. You see, mistakes are a normal part of our lives, and we should look at them as being our friends rather than our foes. If we learn from our blunders, we will be wiser the next time we attempt the task. It is a mistake not to learn from our mistakes. We must recognize that mistakes are not final, and go forth from where we fell. The only person who doesn't fail is the one who doesn't try, and that is the biggest mistake of all. Life is not life unless you are making mistakes. If you are not double-dribbling occasionally, it's simply because you are not in the game. So the next time you hear me, or anyone else, say *"I thought I was wrong once, but I was mistaken!"* just know that we were mistaken, yet again.

A Spanish proverb says, *"He is always right who suspects that he makes mistakes."* A mistake is OK unless you allow it to destroy your belief in yourself. Learn from it, and go forth better prepared for the next lesson. Remember, even the surest of feet slip occasionally. However, when falling, remember to fall forward - that way you're a bit ahead of where you went down.

Life is not life unless you are making mistakes."

Few things are done perfectly on the first attempt. Do not allow that to prevent you from trying again. For if that was the rule we adopted for all of life, none of us would have ever learned to walk. When faced with the fear of making a mistake, we should ask our self, "What is the worst thing that could happen if I fail?" and if you can survive in bearing the consequences, I say, "Go for it!" For every "coat of success" has some "threads of failure" woven within. And I must say, "You look very dapper in that new jacket."

People are not remembered for the times they failed but for the times they succeeded. The number of successes goes up in direct proportion to the number of failures. Failure should be looked at as just another way that did not work and help us realize we are one step closer to success. However, we must accept responsibility for our mistakes and vow to the best of our ability not to make the same mistake again. There is an old saying that says, *"Fool me once, shame on you; fool me twice, shame on me."* To prevent yourself from making the same mistake twice, learn the lesson taught from the first. A man who forgets his umbrella twice cannot blame the rain when he gets wet the second time.

"Mistakes are simply the fee we must pay to be a *life* member."

B.C. Forbes once remarked, *"The man who has done his level best, and who is conscious that he has done his best, is a success, even thought the world may write him down as a failure."* Better is the one who has made mistakes than the one who has never learned to live. The foundation on which success is built is laid with the boulders of blunder, and held together with the mortar of mistakes. Our mistakes are simply the means by which we reach our destination. Failure may not be sweet; that is not saying it has to be bitter. When we lose, we need to say to ourselves, "So what if I didn't win? At least I was in the running!"

Mistakes are simply the fee we must pay to be a "life-member." We must stop beating up ourselves over past failures. "Excusitis" is a disease that often infects failure. A mistake is not a failure but serves as evidence that someone had the courage to attempt something. There is an old Texas saying that, I feel, sums it up eloquently:

"It doesn't matter how much milk you have spilled in the past, just as long as you still have your cow." If you discover that you messed up, and you do not attempt to correct your mistake, you messed up again! In the game of life, one thing about it is that none of us has the pressure of an undefeated season. However, to be defeated while doing good is still a win.

A failure does not mean we are defeated - delayed maybe, but not defeated! Failure is not final; it simply offers a new starting point for the next attempt. When a mistake convinces you that it is hopeless to try again, have the courage to stand up and call it a liar to its face! To persist is to guarantees success. Winston Churchill once said, *"Success is going from failure to failure without loss of enthusiasm."* The only feasible option available to someone who has been knocked down is to rise yet again. When mistakes steal our confidence to try again, they have succeeded in defeating us.

It is easier to forgive **many** mistakes made by others than it is to forget **one** of our own. To have the nerve to admit a mistake, and learn the lesson from it, is to be better for experiencing it. People would have a much better chance of learning from their mistakes if they would take the time to do a thorough examination of them before they try to bury them from the sight of others.

"Don't be afraid to enter the game."

A surgeon was washing up after an operation and was asked by one of his cohorts, *"Hey doc, how did the appendectomy go?"* The doctor answered; *"Appendectomy? I thought it was an autopsy."* The lesson to be learned is that education is the best insurance against making mistakes.

How much more rewarding it is to be a part of the winning team than it is to be simply a fan. Don't be afraid to enter the game. It is better to have played the game and lost, than not to have played the game at all. Few things can bring a person back in touch with reality like a good whoopin'! I know that is the truth because *"I thought I was wrong once, but I was mistaken!"*

*****

"You my brothers, were called to be free. But do not use your freedom to indulge the sinful nature; rather serve one another in love. The entire law is summed up in a single command: "Love your neighbor as yourself." [Galatians 5:13-15]

The Land of Opportunity

⌣∴⌣

Most of us have heard the United States referred to as "The Land of Opportunity." I say that no matter what land you live in, **it** is **your** land of opportunity. The person who says, "Poor little old me," comes to the end of their life and realizes, "Me old, little and poor!" Stop whining about what you do not have and start using what you do. You will discover unlimited opportunities. Start with something possible, dress it in the robe of persistence, and crown it with the halo of hope. The result is opportunity.

Opportunities are omnipresent, but sometimes they like to play "hide and seek." You will most often find that opportunities must be searched for because they come knocking only on occasion. Sometimes opportunity is mistaken as misfortune, and it takes a person with vision to uncover the truth. If opportunity seems to never visit your place, take the liberty to go calling on it. Don't worry, it's at home. Keep knocking until it answers!

Every situation holds some opportunity for good. The problem is that most people think of opportunity only in terms of monetary gain. Opportunities to show love or to develop relationships are priceless, and they offer rewards money cannot buy.

"Every situation holds some opportunity for good."

Opportunity does not come to you who waits; it waits for you who come! If the door of opportunity closes, look for windows! Winston Churchill said, *"An optimist sees opportunity in every calamity; a pessimist sees calamity in every opportunity."* Viewing difficulties as the enemy can paralyze a person with fear. Seeing them as opportunities offers the chance to walk first and then run. Remember, an opportunity that appears small may only be the sprout of what is to become a towering tree. If we can train ourselves to take advantage of small opportunities, we will soon be presented with larger ones. Each day comes with loads of opportunity. Pity the man too busy to take advantage.

Many people are envious of other's opportunities, but their envy blinds them to their own. Opportunity in a neighbor's life is often mistaken as luck. If you want to be a "successful failure," do not answer the door when opportunity knocks. Opportunity will always be there for the one who is willing to look and labor. Opportunity seldom has a nametag, so you may have to ask its name. Make up your mind to look for opportunity, and if you don't find it, make it! If you should find an opportunity that you cannot use, share it with a friend. However, don't get angry when he benefits.

"Opportunity will always be there for the one who is willing to look and labor."

A quote by Orison Sweet Marden goes like this; *"The golden opportunity you are seeking is in yourself. It is not in your environment; it is not in luck or chance, or the help of others; it is in yourself alone."* But so many people will spend their entire life looking for excuses and reasons to explain their lot in life, or the fact that they don't have a lot at all. The person who is willing to look for opportunity is the same one who will make it if he does not find it. Excuses are a dime a dozen, and one will never get rich trying to sell them.

Many people think of opportunity as something for which you must be willing to relocate to find, but many times it is in your own back yard. If you don't find it there, check out front!

Why is it that opportunity knocks only once but temptation kicks the door down? It could be because we are always on the lookout for temptation, and overlooking opportunity.

*****

"Ask and it will be given to you; seek and you will find; knock and the door will be opened to you. For everyone who asks receives; he who seeks finds; and to him who knocks, the door will be opened." [Matthew 7:7-8]

You want It When?

My brother-in-law once told me that I was the most impatient person he knew. I told him he just did not know enough people. However, when I stop to consider his charge, if I found myself sitting on the jury, I would probably have to vote "guilty" as well. Patience may be a virtue, but in most lives it's an option rather than standard equipment. I believe, though, it is something that can be obtained if we are willing to shift the focus from ourselves and try to see things from the other person's point of view. I am still a work in progress, but I am getting tired of waiting!

"Wisdom and patience share the same family tree."

Sometimes patience leaves a nasty taste in the mouth, but the nourishment gained is worth more than the yuck. If we follow a daily diet of patience, self-control and understanding, we can have a body of contentment. We generally produce pounds of patience in areas of personal interest and little or none in the interests of others.

Did you know that wisdom and patience share the same family tree? A person may be well outfitted with the latest fashions but be perceived as a pauper unless patience plays its part. If a life is built around blocks of patience, happiness will be a regular guest. Patience is the ability to sit silently when you feel like standing and shouting.

Patience without preparation looks remarkably like laziness. A teacher who lacks patience teaches little. There is a thin line between being patient and being afraid to react; however, you will know when you cross it, as your peace will be replaced with worry. It seems that when we sit and watch in anticipation without diligently preparing for the arrival, time drags on relentlessly. Excellence takes time but can be realized if we are patient enough and industrious enough.

A Christian cannot present a convincing case for Christ without patience in his words and actions. Sometimes when we pray for patience, God sends it disguised as an irritation. Patience is a masterpiece that increases in value as time marches on. We have no right to demand patience from others if we do not offer it in return. The greatest men of action can benefit tremendously from having men of patience with them to help fight the battle. For few awards are presented to those who lack patience and persistence.

"Patience is a masterpiece that increases in value as time marches on."

An old Chinese proverb says, *"One moment of patience may ward off great disaster; one moment of impatience may ruin a whole life."* How many of us wish we could pull a couple of "do-overs" out of a bag and change something that occurred in our past? Most times an ounce of patience carries more weight than a pound of wisdom, but with both combined we can change our world. React too soon and you may very well be caught in a snare; wait too long and you find what you were looking for is gone. Wisdom knows when to be patient and when to take action. Patience teamed with persistence can pull most any load.

The folly of youth is often mistaken as lack of experience, when lack of patience is the real culprit. A life without patience is like a boat without water. It may be nice to look at, but the pleasure for which it was created is missing. With patience, mountains can be moved with a teaspoon. Patience must be a daily practice; a study from which we never graduate.

If any relationship is to flourish, it must be bathed in love, dusted with the talc of trust, and pampered with patience. If any of these three ingredients is missing, those involved in the relationship will find the time together far short of satisfying.

Anyone else feeling the need for a bath?

*****

"Consider it pure joy, my brothers, whenever you face trials of many kinds, because you know that the testing of your faith develops perseverance. Perseverance must finish its work so that you may be mature and complete, not lacking anything." [James 1:2-4]

Can I Get A Peace Of That Action?

꒦꒷

All of us have probably at some time in our life heard about or saw some deal that we thought we would like to take advantage of, and wondered if we might be able to get a piece of the action. It could have been a hot stock tip, or your favorite dessert sitting on the counter. Whatever the situation, you had a feeling that your life would have more joy in it if you could just get your fair share. However, that hot stock tip can land you in jail if you are not careful (If you don't believe me, ask Martha), and that pie which you thought was pecan ends up being mincemeat. Sometimes, things end up not being as appealing as they first seemed to be. Now if similar situations in your life have left you a bit skeptical, relax. I have got a deal for you!

"What," you may be asking, "could be so tantalizing that I just have to take advantage of it?" And my final answer would be, **"Peace."** Oh, what some would pay to have this luxury as part of their life! However, peace is not for sale, even though it still must be bought through our willingness to pay the price of unselfishness and unconditional love. So go ahead and ask, *"Can I get a peace of that action?"* and my response will be, "I thought you'd never ask!" The shop is open for business. Joy to the world!

"Opposing wills are what creates enemies."

Peace will not be present when we try to force our beliefs on others. We must allow them the freedom to be themselves, and thus express their love and peace in their own unique way. Opposing wills are what creates enemies. When we can agree on common ground, peace will begin to take root. We must exert every effort not to be understood, but to understand! We need to focus on the things we have in common, and not on our differences, if we are striving for peace. When we can adopt a view that sees our neighbor's misfortune as being our own, we will be more empathetic and willing to help in any way we can.

We must allow the "Golden Rule" to be our basis for making decisions about others, for if we do, we will find ourselves inching closer to the palace of peace. The *Power of Love* and the *Love of Power* are at different ends of the seesaw; one is love for others, and one is love for self. To make the world a more peaceful place, begin with yourself by looking out for the wants and needs of others before your own. For peace to exist, we must be willing to give and take. Peace is never a one-way street, but requires willingness from both directions. Selfishness must be put to bed if you wish to enjoy your visit with peace.

Mother Teresa was surely blessed with a special wisdom in regards to peace. She said, *"If we have no peace, it is because we have forgotten that we belong to each other."* The reason for peace is the same reason for love, because it is the right thing to do! However, for peace to prevail, the rules must be justice and righteousness for everyone involved. Trying to obtain peace without God in the picture is like trying to photograph the Grand Canyon while vacationing in Florida. It ain't going to happen!

"When love leaves, it takes peace with it."

When love leaves, it takes peace with it. Sometimes we must be willing to make changes in our self before we can hope to see a change in others. Consideration for other's feelings will cause us to think twice before we act in haste, and that pause could be the one that refreshes us with peace. Peace and harmony are both children of the love family.

You may be able to force a desired action from another, but this is not the way to make a friend. You cannot force love, but love can force you. Be willing to give into the pressure, for the victory of war has its spoils, but the victory of peace brings unending rewards. Peace must be a compromise because if one side gives all and the other offers nothing, there will be no peace. With peace, the proof is in the pudding!

War and peace can dwell in the same heart, but it depends on the priorities as to which prevails. Shame on the mind that dreams war instead of peace, for it has allowed its focus to be distracted. War is dependent on the willingness of people to fight one another, just as peace is dependent on their decision to go against that will. It has been said that being ready for war is a great preserver of peace, but I might add that being ready for peace is the beginning of the end of war. Preparing for peace means making sure the 'Welcome" mat is out, the door is unlocked, and the light is on for our honored guest, peace. Though the desire for peace is no guarantee for its presence, it does offer the hope that the possibility exists. We must not only be willing to talk of peace, we must be willing to walk in peace as well. To find peace with the world, you must first find peace with yourself.

"A certain amount of ugly must be present before beauty's full potential can be recognized."

St. Francis of Assisi put it as well as anyone could have when he said, *"Lord, make us instruments of thy peace. Where there is hatred, let us sow love; where there is injury, pardon; where there is discord, union; where there is doubt, faith; where there is despair, hope; where there is darkness, light; where there is sadness, joy."*

Each of these steps can ensure us of "peace on earth." Now peace may be a team effort, but it is perfected by playing a man-to-man defense. Being a team player means being unselfish and willing to take whatever steps necessary to win the hearts of others through peace.

A certain amount of ugly must be present before beauty's full potential can be recognized. That is why peace looks so good in the shadows of discord. Are you ready to admit that your life has had more ugly than you can handle? If so, go ahead and ask, *"Can I get a peace of that action?"* You know the answer, "Yes"!

*****

"For, whoever would love life and see good days must keep his tongue from evil and his lips from deceitful speech. He must turn from evil and do good; he must seek peace and pursue it."
[1 Peter 3:10-11]

Oh, Boy, What A Waste!

Have you ever had the chance to know someone who had so much potential and yet never took advantage of it? You have to shake your head and wonder why. Why would they allow such natural talent to go to waste, when they could have not only made such a positive impact on their own life but on the lives of others? We all have the potential to do more than we think we can. Therefore, we must stop limiting ourselves by our thoughts. So what if we end up falling short of absolute success? We will have progressed far more than if we had not attempted something big.

Every person has seeds of greatness that lie buried within; some never realize maturity because they are neglected. Full potential is not realized in one big step but in the succession of many small ones leading in the same direction. Do not sell yourself short by thinking you are not capable of achieving something, at least not until you have given it an all out attempt. No one limits us like we limit ourselves. Please, do not allow yourself to be one of the people of whom others say, *"Oh, boy, what a waste!"* when they speak of your potential.

"No one limits us like we limit ourselves."

If we were capable of seeing the person we could be, if our full potential were utilized, we probably would not recognize us. One time George Bernard Shaw was asked who he would most like to be, if he had the chance to be anyone else. His response is a classic. He said, *"I would most like to be the man George Bernard Shaw could have been, but never was."* If we were truly honest with ourselves, most of us would answer the same way. For to come to the end of our life and realize we had become all we could have, this would have been a full life. Greatness comes to those who concentrate on doing the best they can under any set of circumstances. Do your best to break through self-imposed barriers and you will realize what your potential truly is. A soul that is designed to fly will never be content walking!

Do not allow yourself or anyone else to impose mind boundaries on you, for just beyond is where you want to be. We must take advantage of opportunities when they present themselves because if we do not, they will soon be gone. Every day offers the possibility of new potential, and we should not limit ourselves by the memories of what we have or have not accomplished up to this point. We need to evaluate every experience to understand how it may lead to a higher ground.

One of the biggest challenges most of us face is realizing who we are inside, and then allowing that to become reality. If your friends tell you that you cannot do something, you need to look for another group of friends. Do not allow the small thinking of others to stunt your growth as a person. Much potential is never realized because of the adverse effect negative comments have on it. Just because something has never been done before does not mean that it cannot be done. Look at the example of Roger Bannister, and how he broke a barrier that most believed to be impossible - running a mile in less than four minutes. Many doctors believed a man's heart would literally explode if such strenuous exertion was demanded, yet Bannister believed that he could do it. After he accomplished this amazing feat back in 1954, countless thousands have since done the same thing. The only way to discover the unexpected is to expect it!

We must realize that the world does not end at the point where your vision stops. You will discover that if you go as far as you can see, you will be able to see farther still. It is the same with our potential in that if we do all we can, we discover that now we can see the possibility of going farther. Attitude is a major factor in reaching our full potential. If we think we cannot do something, our mind will come up with at least a dozen reasons why we can't but on the other hand, if we tell ourselves we can, we will look for all the possible ways to achieve it.

> **"Do not allow the small thinking of others
> to stunt your growth as a person."**

Do not be afraid to question yourself because this may lead you to see ways to improve your performance. Develop your talents to be all you can be, and then you will be pleasantly surprised to discover that you have new talents that are waiting to be utilized. Do not allow reality to prevent you from redesigning reality. Dare to dream! In so doing, you create new worlds of possibilities. To do more, expect more!

You can only begin from where you are and move forward, taking an inventory of what you have to work with, and progressing from there to your fullest extent. It seems that potential is more fully realized in the lives of the motivated. Therefore, we need to concentrate on doing what we can to make sure we keep ourselves surrounded by positive people and the encouraging feedback they supply. We need to concentrate on the purpose at hand, for through focusing our thoughts and energy, we can realize our potential.

> **"To do more, expect more!"**

To be sure of a miserable life, make plans to not live up to your potential. For to come to the end of our life and realize that we have not even attempted to do something we always wanted to, is clearly to have failed. Such is the case with this book. I have dreamed for countless years to write this book but never took action to see it become a reality. I told my wife that I did not want to find myself on my deathbed, wishing that I had at least tried to put my thoughts down on paper. Not that this will ever be a best-seller, but I know my life without it would have been less than what I thought it could have been. I encourage taking a serious look at your own life and seeing if there are any unfulfilled dreams in your "bucket list" that may still be lingering there. If so, do all you possibly can to make them become reality. I can guarantee you that you do not want to look at your life and say, *"Oh, boy, what a waste!"*

*****

"I can do everything through him who gives me strength."
[Philippians 4:13]

Now That Is Powerful!

S ome may believe that the current holder of the "World's Strongest Man" contest would be the most powerful as well, but common sense would tell us otherwise. Brute strength does not equate to power, except in the world of weights. I would be amiss even to attempt to name the most powerful person in the world today, but I can guarantee you that it is not the same as the WSM champion. The strength of any power is measured by its ability to create change, and the capacity for getting others to participate willingly in the process. Few in the positions of power are as powerful as they imagine, and, likewise, those in subordinate roles are not as weak as they fear. I appreciate the quote from Margaret Thatcher on the subject of power that says, *"Being powerful is like being a lady. If you have to tell people you are, you aren't."* I don't care what others may think of that quote, all I can say is, *"Now that is powerful!"*

You can soon tell what is in the make-up of a person when they are placed in a position of power. It is a fact that not everyone is capable of performing in a position of power. Power carries with it the seeds of construction and the seeds of destruction. If you are in a position of power, you need to make sure you are sowing the seeds that will benefit everyone involved.

**"Power will bring pains with it,
unlike any encountered in a lesser position."**

With power comes the responsibility for the well-being of all who are under your control, plus the loss of liberties. Power will bring pains unlike any encountered in a lesser position. Power must also be accompanied with a love for the truth and a love for the people, or else it will prove unhealthy for everyone. Power will expose a person's true character faster than one can imagine. Happiness is not a natural by-product of power; it comes only with the wisdom of proper handling of power. However, properly used power is an asset in any position of life.

True power does not fear subordinates who flex their muscles and exert their own level of power, for they realize the steps necessary to accomplish the task at hand. Generally speaking, the one with the most power is the same as the one with the most accurate information. Knowledge has the potential for power, but wisdom in how best to apply the knowledge is a prerequisite. Ideas have power, but the might lays with the one who has the ability to put the ideas into action. For the best plan in the world will not work until you work the plan. A thought, however, contains all the power necessary to start the wheels turning.

Power in the wrong hands can be devastating indeed, as can be seen through different incidences throughout history. Before you vote for someone or something, be sure you can endure the consequences without them causing a fatality. Power can be as intoxicating as the strongest drink, and can destroy a person just as surely as alcoholism. A person in a power position must make sure they do not allow it to go to their head. A person who is consumed with power will soon be consumed by it.

"A person who is consumed with power will soon be consumed by it."

Eventually to find yourself in a position of power you need to take advantage of every opportunity offered to learn more in regards to your business. Even a person with limited knowledge will still have power over those who have none. Power is not so much the ability to hit hard, or even often, but to hit the mark squarely.

To have the power to abuse but never using it is the true test. It is not so much that power will make good men bad, but that good men will abuse the power entrusted to them. Those who strive for power to exalt self will make poor leaders. Access to power must be denied to men who are in love with it, and what it can mean for personal good. Lord Acton once said, *"Power tends to corrupt, and absolute power corrupts absolutely."* No person is wise enough to be trusted with absolute power.

Power is to protect and promote, not harass and harm. Power without humility can cause danger to all. A good example is more powerful than words alone. If we are hoping to be placed in a position of power, we must be willing to walk the walk as well as talk the talk. Confined power is useful and beneficial, but when allowed to get out of control, it can cause utter destruction.

"It is true that sometimes the hardest thing to control is self."

Each person can have more power than is imaginable. The challenge comes in discovering the most productive way to utilize it. Most people only use a small percentage of their ability and thus allow the remainder to go to waste. It is true that sometimes the hardest thing to control is self.

It sometimes takes a greater power to contend with the person in the power position than to be in the position your self. A leader's perception of power will determine their effectiveness. A person with newly gained power will have a tendency to be a stickler for the rules, at least until he learns that even he cannot follow all of them. At that point, you will begin to see some easing up on the regulations. A fool with power is an accident waiting to happen. And with the size of some fools today, all I can say is, *"Now that is powerful!"*

*****

"But I tell you who hear me: Love your enemies, do good to those who hate you, bless those who curse you, pray for those who mistreat you. If someone strikes you on one cheek, turn to him the other also. If someone takes your cloak, do not stop him from taking your tunic.

131

Give to everyone who asks you, and if anyone takes what belongs to you, do not demand it back. Do to others as you would have them do to you." [Luke 6:27-31]

Please Help Me, I'm Falling!

The subject of pride is a touchy one indeed. A person must take pride in their self, but the problem comes in being able to control how it is presented to the world. If one does not take pride in their work, we call him a slacker. However, when someone takes the chance to share what he or she has accomplished, we call him or her a braggart. It is almost enough to make one throw up their hands and say, "What's the use? I cannot win for losing." However, the truth of the matter is that you can win, and the world can be the victor for your triumph. The answer comes in having a realistic view of self, and not thinking you are something that you are not. The Bible tells us that pride comes before a downfall, so we need to be very careful in how we live our lives in regards to our self-image. When we start thinking we are something because of our accomplishments, we might as well go ahead and say, *"Please help me, I'm falling!"*

Pride is a deceiver in that it leads one to believe he or she is deserving of praise that really belongs to another. Pride is the culprit that leads to most mistakes. Our wrong thinking causes us to make decisions, which are anything but wise. Upon close examination, it will be discovered that most mistakes are built on the foundation of pride. Paul Eldridge is credited with saying, *"Every goose is certain she could lay golden eggs if only properly fed."* Like the geese, we are always anxious to look for someone else to blame our shortcomings on, rather than accepting responsibility ourselves. Arrogance allows the low man on the totem pole to believe he is actually atop, if only the world would get itself upright. To be full of self is to be an empty vessel indeed.

"To be full of self is to be an empty vessel indeed."

Pride is a paradox in that it keeps some from being foolish and yet causes others to be consumed with silliness. The difference lies in the fact that one is of truth and the other of deceit.

Conceit and arrogance are Siamese twins, and the children of pride. We must do our best to separate ourselves from both, and allow humility to adopt us. The key is to possess humility and not be aware of it. For just at the moment when we think we are humble, we are no longer so.

Pride tends to be an obstacle to many because they have their noses stuck up in the air and are watching to see that others are watching them. Just so you know, a head held high and a stuck-up nose is not the same thing.

"Pride is reluctant to take a back seat while humility is just thankful for the ride."

Pride is reluctant to take a back seat; humility is just thankful for the ride. A prideful person is one who believes the world would have suffered had it not been for his or her presence. However, it has been shown that the bigger a person's head, the easier it is to fill the shoes. Prideful people are seldom grateful people, for they always believe they deserve more than what they are being credited for.

The joke is told of the woman who had stopped into a pet shop to see about buying herself a dog. She wanted one of high standards, which she could be proud of, and show off to her neighbors. She insisted that the dog be a pedigree and have papers and the lot. The owner of the shop assured her of the dog's quality by telling her, *"Lady, if this dog could talk, he wouldn't speak to either one of us!"* We need to take caution when we get to thinking we are something that we are not, because pride has a way of making devils out of angels.

We need to be cautious around those who flatter us with their words. Flattery is a fib that tickles the ears of its recipient. Flattery is to the ears of a prideful person as honey is to the tongue of the famished. To relieve the pain of a swelled head, take a daily dose of humility. Humility gives one a proper perspective of self, whereas pride always provides a distorted view.

How nice it would be to have the assurance of anything, equal to the assurance of everything, by a prideful person. There is definitely something wrong with a person who is always right. I have heard it said that the most difficult mental cases to cure are the ones who are crazy about themselves.

Conceit is cocky and may go off at anytime, resulting in wounds to the feelings of others. Conceit is God's gift to little people. Conceit cheats a person of realism and causes them to live in a fantasy world. Mark Twain once said, *"The world owes you nothing; it was here first."* Remembering that fact would allow many to comprehend that what they believe is an open mind is really nothing more than a vacant space.

"Conceit is God's gift to little people."

Many people know they are lost but their pride will not allow them to stop and ask for directions. The "King of Faults" is the one who believes he can do no wrong. However, we must realize that "I" is always in the middle of sin and pride, no matter how you look at it. Man is the only known species of the animal kingdom that gets a swelled head from a pat on the back.

Each of us needs to remember the fact that there is only one God - and it is not us! It is not so much that we need to think less of our self, but that we need to think of our self less. There is a difference, but just in case you didn't know it, repeat after me: *"Please help me I'm falling!"*

*****

"Pride goes before destruction, a haughty spirit before a fall."
[Proverbs 16:18]

Don't Get Your M&M's Confused!

W hen I was a little boy I never had a problem with getting my M&M's confused. But if you know anything about the history of M&M's, you might say, "Well of course not. When you were a little boy, the only kind of M&M's they had was M&M's plain, and they were all brown!" And you know what? You would be right!

But as fate would have it, the Mars Company wasn't satisfied to leave things as they were. In 1954 they introduced M&M peanut; still all brown; but it now gets a bit more complicated in keeping them straight. Then in 1960 they had the audacity to introduce red, green and yellow, to both the plain and peanut versions. Now there are eight varieties to keep track of.

But, oh, no, they didn't stop there. In 1990 they brought out the peanut butter variety; in 1991 it was M&M's almond; in 1999 it was crispy M&M's.

But the proverbial straw that broke the camel's back was in 1996 when they introduced the M&M "minis." That did it! How in the world could anybody keep from getting all these M&M's confused?

Now you might say, "Well, how come the mini's gave you so much trouble? Anybody can see that there is a tremendous difference in the size of them!" And I couldn't agree more. But let me ask you a more serious question; "How can we get the M&M's (Majors & Minors) of life so easily confused, when there is such a great difference in the size of them?" I believe we do it on a daily basis. We spend way too much time on the little things (minors) that don't matter, and way too little time on the big things (majors) that shape and make our lives worth living. We need to be aware of how we are doing, and do everything we can to make sure we are not majoring in the minors and minoring in the majors! Keep the main thing the main thing, and don't allow trivial distractions to get you off track.

Without proper priorities, we discover the things we should have done are left undone; and things we should never have attempted are chalked up as experience. Here's one way to determine if you are spending time on the right thing or not: if the activity you're involved in isn't leaving you closer to your goal, you're entertaining the wrong priority. Priorities allow us to realize the greatest possible results for the amount of effort exerted.

Keep the main thing the main thing!

Many times the reason we get our priorities mixed up is because we lose sight of what is really important. It is so easy to get sucked into believing that what the world says is important is important. Often, this is just not the case. The world will tell us that the kind of car we drive and the size of the house we live in determine who or what we are. But when life is analyzed, we discover that few "things" are farther from the truth. What really matters, when all is all said and done, are issues pertaining to the relationships we have with those we love and with whom we associate. The majority of interests or things to which we devote ourselves are only temporary. We should instead invest time, effort and money into developing goals of eternal worth. Many people get near the end of their life and realize they have messed up "big time." Some are so enamored with temporary things that they seldom grasp the importance of the things and great moments they missed out on.

The story is told of a little boy who met his father at the front door one evening when his dad came home from work. The first words out of the son's mouth were, "Dad, how much money do you make an hour?" The father was disturbed by the question and politely told his son it wasn't right to ask someone how much money they made. The little boy was persistent and asked his question again. The father, tired from his day at work and just wanting to relax for a minute or two before supper, finally answered; "Well, if you must know, I make $15.00 an hour." The little boy's face saddened a bit, but then he asked another question; "Dad, can I borrow $1.00?" This infuriated the father and his immediate response was, "Absolutely not! If the only reason you wanted to know how much money I make was so you can borrow some, you can go straight to your room without supper. Go up there and consider what you just did!"

The little boy did as he was told. But after a short while the father got to thinking about his reaction to his son and decided that he had perhaps been too harsh. So he went upstairs to his son's room to offer an apology and ask for forgiveness. He opened the door and found his son sitting on his bed. The father apologized and handed his son a dollar with the explanation that he knew the boy must have a legitimate reason for asking to borrow the money.

At the sight of the dollar, the little boy's demeanor completely changed from somber to jubilation. He threw back his pillow, revealing a wad of money. On seeing the cash, the father once again lost his composure and stated his displeasure that the boy would ask to borrow a dollar when he already had a bunch of money. The little boy's reply brought him to his senses when he explained, "I know, dad. But I only had $14.00 before. Now I have $15.00! Can I buy an hour of your time so we can play together?"

All I can say is "Ouch!" Because I realize that I, too, had my priorities mixed up during our daughter's young years, and therefore she and I missed out on much happiness. I think that is why Harry Chapin's song, *The Cat's In The Cradle*; is so important to me. It reminds me every time I hear it that I need to constantly reevaluate my priorities to make sure I am indeed majoring in the majors and minoring in the minors. I wish for you -and for me- the wisdom to know the difference between them.

Just a word of warning that busyness can cause people to believe they are accomplishing great things, when in reality they are running in place. Activity does not equal accomplishment.

Activity does not equal accomplishment.

After winning the Nobel Peace prize, Mother Teresa made the decision to stop traveling to accept any more recognition because the accolades were starting to interfere with and affect the quality of her work. She realized her priority was to help the poor people of Calcutta, not make speeches and accept awards. If all of us could be so insightful, the world would be better for it.

To help yourself determine what your priorities really are, ask yourself this three-part question; "Where do I spend my time, money and effort?" Your answers will tell you plainly what you are majoring on. A word of caution as I close: "Don't get your M&M's (of life) confused!"

*****

Trust in the Lord with all your heart and lean not on your own under-standing; in all your ways acknowledge Him, and He will make your paths straight." [Proverbs 3:5-6]

When I Get Around To It

I know this will not come as a great surprise to some of you, but this chapter on procrastination is one of the last ones I wrote. It's not that I have been putting it off or anything, it is just because I have not gotten around to it before. It is a little bit like it was when I was in college, knowing that I had a test coming up, and still waiting until the night before to start studying for it. I must admit that I have pulled my fair share of "all-nighters," cramming for tests that I had known about for weeks. I am not sure what makes us do things like that, but I take comfort in knowing that I am not the only one who does. I believe we need to help each other with overcoming this bad habit of procrastination. Therefore, the next time you hear me say, *"When I get around to it..."* give me a friendly push in the right direction. Then you and I will do it together - first thing tomorrow!

Most of the tasks that we procrastinate about could be over with in the time we spend worrying about them. We need to just make up our mind and take action. Before we know, it will be finished, and we will realize that it was not as bad as we had feared. If we put off until tomorrow what we should be doing today, tomorrow will be too full to manage. The only things you should put off until tomorrow, are the things you don't have any business doing in the first place.

"...Procrastination is the devil's chloroform."

I read somewhere that procrastination is the devil's chloroform. It does have the tendency to make us live in an unconscious state, unaware of the consequences that delay may bring with it. Delay can be deadly if we do not take advantage of the opportunities we have today because they may not return tomorrow. Satan could care less about what you are "going to do" but trembles about your actions of today. The one who ignores the present throws away the future. The fool is the king of tomorrow, for tomorrow never comes.

If we are not careful, the sweet "by and by" will soon become the bitter "never did." Many people are guilty of putting off until tomorrow the things that they should have done *yesterday.* I wish I could tell you that things become easier when you put them on hold, but the opposite is true. If we continue to put off the little things that we should be doing, they will soon create an insurmountable mountain. The fact is, the longer you delay in dealing with a duty, the more difficult it becomes. A procrastinator is a person with a big "wait" problem.

Not many songs really speak to me, but one that did a few years ago was **Live Like You Were Dying** by Tim McGraw. I think the message is one that we need to hear on a daily basis. Life is short, and if we continue to put off doing things that we would love to do until we get around to doing them, most will go undone. None of us is guaranteed another tomorrow, so do yourself a favor and take action on fulfilling any unfulfilled dreams that you may have. Stop procrastinating. If you don't, "one of these days" will soon become "none of these days." Procrastination is a thief that will hold you up in broad daylight!

"Be sure your "but" doesn't get in your way of doing."

The fear of making a wrong decision can cause us to put things off as long as possible. However, many times the consequences of making a bad decision are easier to deal with than those caused by waiting. Surely you have heard, *"The road to hell is paved with good intentions."* It took me years to understand the full meaning of this, but now I know; it makes no difference in the world what I plan to do! If I don't take action on my intent, I would be better off not having it in the first place. Putting off until another time has proved to be the death of many worthwhile works. The words "one of these days" is a crutch for the procrastinator and does nothing toward getting the tasks at hand completed.

Many are they who live in the fantasy world of "I'll be happy when..." However, I discovered long ago that if I wait for something to come along to make me happy, it will never come. Each of us has a choice to make - wait for something to happen to make you happy, or decide to be happy today. Do not wait; start today! To ensure that your life doesn't bomb, join the TNT crew - "**T**oday, **N**ot **T**omorrow."

If you hear someone say, "Wait just a little while," pay close attention to the clock. For a little while can soon turn into never, and before you know it, time has passed you by. Life does not slow down just because you do!

"Life does not slow down just because you do!"

I heard a joke sometime back about a guy who was rummaging through some items in the attic when he came across his old letter jacket from high school. In searching the pockets, he discovered an unclaimed shoe repair ticket almost ten years old. The next morning he decided to satisfy his curiosity as to whether or not the store was still in business. To his surprise, it was. When he presented his claim check, the proprietor took it, walked into the back room for a while, then came back out, and said, "They should be ready by next Tuesday."

WARNING: Be sure your "but" doesn't get in your way of doing!

Time cannot be managed, only spent. We must plan wisely on how to make the best use of it while we have it. Never getting around to taking action has caused hunger in a starving world. So make up your mind to take action now, and never again use the lame excuse of, *"When I get around to it..."*

*****

"Now listen, you who say, 'Today or tomorrow we will go to this or that city, spend a year there, carry on business and make money.' Why you do not even know what will happen tomorrow. What is your life? You are a mist that appears for a little while and then vanishes. Instead, you ought to say, 'If it is the Lord's will, we will live and do this or that.' As it is, you boast and brag. All such boasting is evil. Anyone, then, who knows the good he ought to do and doesn't do it, sins." [James 4:13-17]

Life Is A Risky Business

If you really stop and think about it, every aspect of our lives is somewhat of a risk, is it not? If we get out of bed, we risk an endless list of happenings. If we stay in bed, we risk the chance of losing our ability to get out of bed. So what do we do? My advice is to live your life to its fullest, and do so by being willing to take the calculated risks that will allow you to really live. So what if you fall flat on your face sometimes? You will be wiser for having the experience. As long as you can withstand the worst of the possible consequences and still walk away, go for it! Because after all, *"Life is a risky business."*

Taking risks is not the same as blindly jumping into a cage before checking to see if the lion is at home. Always do your homework so you can be well prepared to face the challenge. One of Mary Kay's slogans to live by is, *"Bite off more than you can chew - then chew it!"* The greatest mystery for all is, "What could have been if I had been willing to risk more?" The things people regret the most are the things they never tried. The only way to discover just how far you can go is to risk going farther than you have ever been before. Life is made sweeter by the risks we take and the rewards they bring.

**"The things people regret the most
are the things they never tried."**

The turtle would be forced to lead a dull life unless he was willing to stick his neck out occasionally. Do not allow precautions to prevent you from being all you can be. Sometimes the biggest risk lies in the unwillingness to take a risk. Great accomplishments are the result of great risks. How will you ever know what you can do without first taking a risk? To win, one must risk losing.

If you keep on doing what you have always been doing, you are going to keep getting what you have always gotten. If you are not satisfied with that, then take a risk and do something differently.

Our country is the result of risk-takers. It is our duty to leave the world a better place for those who come after, and the only way this can be accomplished is through risk-taking. Those who are not willing to take risks are slaves to their precautions. A Japanese proverb reads, *"Unless you enter the tiger's den, you cannot take the cubs."* Being willing to take a risk in no way means that fear is not present. However, you must take control of your fear and proceed, knowing that you have done your homework, and are ready to face the adventure that accompanies the risk. Not to risk is not to live.

"Not to risk is not to live."

If you are waiting for all risks to be eliminated before getting on with your life, you can forget that - it is not going to happen! To gain without risk is likened to winning a race you never entered. All progress carries some level of risk. Nothing ventured, nothing gained. There must be a balance between caution and risk, but it requires risk to know what that balance is. Risk-takers are not afraid to make mistakes, and therefore they progress more rapidly than their cautious co-workers. Sometimes the best educator is the failure a person encounters from taking a risk. Learn from your mistakes and then move forward, wiser than before.

If we only knew the outcome before the undertaking, life would be surer for sure, but the adventure would be lost. It is a fact that you will never accomplish anything you never try. To play it safe does not mean that you take no risks. Calculated risks are wise, whereas rash actions are foolish. No one tests the depth of the water with both feet. The rule to look before you leap will at least give you an idea of the size of the risk. Remember, the level of risk is reduced when the level of preparation is increased.

If you are not willing to fail big, do not expect to win big. For the rewards offered by opportunity will be measured by the same yardstick as the risks involved. No guts, no glory!

"No risk = no hope!"

The story is told of a general who would always offer the prisoners who were sentenced to die a choice. He gave them the opportunity to choose between a firing squad and whatever lay behind a big black door. More often than not, the prisoners would choose the known to the unknown, and opt for the quick death offered by the firing squad. The irony is that the big black door led to freedom. Yet the element of the unknown prevented the men from taking the risk that would lead to life.

Sometimes we must risk more than we think we can endure to discover treasures we never knew existed. If we have any hope of success, we must be willing to risk. No risk = no hope!

In the world of business, it has been said there are three stages that one most go through. First, there is the "risk-taker" stage where the willingness to take risks and try anything is prevalent. Next comes the "caretaker" stage that happens after some success has been achieved, and protection is the goal. Lastly comes the "undertaker" stage, the one where complacency sets in and eventually the decline that leads to death. I believe these three stages are often not only true for business but apply to many areas of our lives as well.

My challenge to each of you is this: if we are not living in stage one, do whatever possible to get there, and then live life as it was meant to be lived. If we wait until all the lights are green, we will never leave home and therefore miss out on this adventure we call life. Saddle up your horses; we've got a trail to blaze! And we all know going in, *"Life is a risky business."*

*****

"Anyone who loves his father or mother more than me is not worthy of me; anyone who loves his son or daughter more than me is not worthy of me; and anyone who does not take his cross and follow me is not worthy of me. Whoever finds his life will lose it, and whoever loses his life for my sake will find it." [Matthew 10:37-39]

Find A Need And Fill It

W hen I think about a modern example of what it means to be a servant, and have a true servant's heart, my thoughts most often go to that of Mother Teresa. Before her death in 1997, she literally gave her life to serve the poor people of Calcutta.

One incident that I read about was when she was wrapping up the wounds of a leper, covering the gaping hole that existed where once the man's nose was. She was being watched by an American tourist, who finally asked if he might take a picture of her doing what she did best. She granted permission. After the man was finished taking his photographs, he said, "I wouldn't do what you are doing for $10 million!" Mother Teresa looked up from finishing her work and replied, "Neither would I, my friend. Neither would I!"

The fact of the matter is that service, in the true sense, is something you cannot put a price tag on, and wouldn't even if you could. You see, it is not about money; it is about finding a need and filling it.

True service comes only when accompanied by sincerity. If your motive for serving is not sincere, it is counterfeit. Not only must we serve in love, we must be adorned with the apron of patience and kindness as well. If we serve in such a hurry that the recipient is shorted of personal contact, full service has not been supplied. It is not as important *where* you serve as it is in *how* you serve.

**"If your motive for serving is anything but sincere,
it is a counterfeit."**

Granted, you miss out on the blessing of personal contact that I mentioned in the paragraph above, but to be able to serve the need of another, and be able to remain anonymous, is one of life's greatest treasures. Service in a just cause will inspire and enlighten a person to want to do more, and will bring joy in the process. We must answer the question, "Whom will we serve?" If it is self, our lives will only be a shadow of what life is meant to be. If it is others, it will be everything.

In days of old, the number of servants he had may have measured a man's level of success. Today, and, truthfully, forever, the true measure is more by how many people he has served. For a life to have meaning, it has to find a way to serve. Service is our way of paying back what we owe to the world. To be willing to serve is noble; to serve is righteous. If you want to bless yourself, bless others. If you want to live a life of misery, spend your life thinking of ways to get others to serve you.

"For a life to have meaning, it has to find a way to serve."

No matter what talent we have been blessed with, we should put it to work in serving others, and not bury it deep within our selfish selves. Greatness is achieved through forgetting self and seeing how we can enrich the lives of others. If your chief concern is building up service to others, your bank account will take care of itself.

A quote that I came across from Orison Swett Marden in regard to what service is all about is, *"He is the richest man who enriches his country most; in whom the people feel richest and proudest; who gives himself with his money; who opens the doors of opportunity widest to those around him; who is ears to the deaf, eyes to the blind, and feet to the lame. Such a man makes every acre of land in his community worth more, and makes richer every man who lives near him."*

We each need to ask if that can be said about us. Are the lives around us enriched because of our service to others, or do we simply exist?

In business, if you are more concerned about making a profit than about serving the customer, you will find that you are in for a rough time. To build a business, you need to be more concerned with what you give than with what you get. For, if you take care of the first, the second will be taken care of as well. A life of plenty begins with finding your area of service and doing your best to fulfill it to the level of making others feel important and pampered.

"To face death with no record of ways in which you served your fellow man is a true sign that you never really lived."

Money and a wealth of material things cannot bring true joy as much as finding a need in someone else's life and fulfilling it. The highest honor one can receive is to be called "servant." To face death with no record of ways in which you served your fellow man is a true sign that you never really lived. Indeed, a person who thinks only of self is wrapped in a very small package.

To complain of no joy in life is, I think, to say you are too busy or just not interested enough to serve others. No matter what we do for a living, we are in the service business. Until you find a need and fill it, you have just…existed. Only after serving do you really begin to know and enjoy the good things of life.

The true measure of a person's life is determined only by the times he has benefited others. Each of us can only hope to forget ourselves more, and to remember others during these times. The real Medal of Honor goes to the one who is the servant of others.

If you were arrested for being a "servant," would there be enough evidence to convict you? If not, all I can suggest is that you *"Find a need and fill it!"*

*****

"Do nothing out of selfish ambition or vain conceit, but in humility consider others better than yourselves. Each of you should look not only to your own interests, but also to the interests of others." [Philippians 2:3-4]

Smile; It Will Increase Your Face Value!

～∶～

One of my favorite things to do when my wife goes shopping is to go with her and then participate by watching people. I know I am not alone when I say I would much rather find a seat and observe, than to go into a store and pretend to be interested in something when I am not.

When I do this, I never cease to be amazed at the number of people who look like they have been weaned on a pickle. They have the sourest look on their faces and act like Hinny Penny just told them the sky is falling. Sometimes I have to stop myself from getting up and following them and telling them to *"Smile; it will increase your face value!"* But then again, if everyone were smiling as they walked by me, after I checked to make sure my fly wasn't open, I would take a trip to the nearest mirror to see what's so funny. Because even though a smile is the universal language, so few seem to comprehend.

A smile on the face is simply a reflection of love in the heart.

A smile will do more to improve your looks than the best plastic surgeon could ever hope to. A smile on the face is simply a reflection of love in the heart. And in like manner, it is impossible to have a smile in your heart and not let it show on your face.

153

I can't explain it, but when you wear a smile, your whole personality improves. A smile makes the face look brighter and adds warmth to the heart. It's also nice to know that it will go with any outfit, and it never goes out of style. A man in rags with a smile on his face is better dressed than the one adorning a thousand-dollar outfit with a frown. A wardrobe is never complete without a smile. So wear a smile everyday; you can never wear it out!

With the cost of everything going up these days, it's nice to know that the cost of a smile never goes up, and the value of one never goes down. A smile is God's way of showing the world the natural beauty of a person without the need for cosmetics. A smile is a natural by-product of both love and kindness.

A smile is a natural by-product of both love and kindness.

The story is told of a cowboy who happened upon a city slicker as he was saddling his horse. The cowboy informed the dude that he was putting the saddle on backward. The greenhorn's reply was, "You think you're so smart. You don't even know which way I'm going!" Well, what are you smiling at? It makes sense to me!

It is nearly impossible to wear a smile on your outside and not feel better on the inside. You have a choice to either grin and bear it or smile and change it. The choice is yours. However, you can rest assured if you find someone who is smiling when things are going wrong, chances are they've figured out somebody to blame. Or they may know that the insurance will cover it! Either way, I guess it is reason enough to grin a bit.

I read an article about an interview process held by Holiday Inn. They were interviewing some 5,000 people to fill only 500 jobs. Anyone who smiled fewer than four times during the interview was automatically disqualified. My question for you is, "Would you have made the final cut?"

I have found few things in this world that fits the "One-size-fits-all" category, but a smile surely does. It may be only a small investment, but a smile can reward you with great returns. It is a magnet that draws others to you, and makes them want whatever it is you have. A smile seems to make the bumps of life a bit easier to tolerate. And everyone knows we could all benefit from a smoother ride.

I don't know about you, but I have found that it is easier to smile when I know someone cares about me. And many times the way I know they care is because of the smile they have on their face when they meet me. Yet a smile doesn't necessarily need to be seen to be effective; it improves the worth and feeling of the one who wears it.

Akin to the old chicken and egg question, is this one, "Are you smiling because you're happy, or are you happy because you're smiling?" My answer would be the same as it would for the chickens and eggs. "Does it really matter?" I don't think it does, as long as both are alive and well.

A smile is the shortest distance between two people.

Have you ever found yourself in a party, job or other situation where there were a number of people around you, but you knew absolutely no one? I have, and I must admit that it is not the most pleasant scenario. However, I have discovered that a smile is usually strong enough to break the ice and will get another to open up when I take the initiative. A smile is the shortest distance between two people. So remember, the next time you find yourself in such a condition, smile. It will either get the person talking to you, or it will make them wonder what you're up to! No matter the outcome, just remember to *"Smile; it will increase your face value!"*

*****

Therefore my heart is glad and my tongue rejoices; my body also will rest secure. [Psalm 16:9]

Stress Is A Mess

Almost half of all adults suffer adverse health effects due to stress. Stress has been linked to all leading causes of death including heart disease, cancer, lung ailments, accidents and suicide. Job stress is estimated to cost U.S. industry $300 billion annually, due to absenteeism, diminished productivity, employee turnover, medical insurance, etc. I must admit that at one time I was a victim of stress and its related symptoms, so I can easily believe the afore-mentioned facts. Due to work pressure, I found myself waking up at 2 a.m. with chest pains and cold sweats, and not being able to go back to sleep. I and anyone else who has been affected by stress would agree that *stress is a mess*! Being a success at stress will lead you to an early grave.

I know some stress is brought on by circumstances over which we have little or no control, but I believe much of it is self-imposed by overestimating the magnitude of our problems. We have a tendency to imagine things as being worse than they are. If we would just take the time to look at the good things in our lives, it would enable us to understand that the good usually far outweighs the bad. Why not take out a pencil and paper and make two lists, the good and bad things in your life. You might be happily surprised.

Being a success at stress will lead you to an early grave.

On the other hand, most of us would probably be unwilling to participate in a group activity where everyone writes all their troubles on a piece of paper, and puts them in a basket. Then everyone draws out someone else's troubles. We soon discover that we don't have to look far to find another who is in worse circumstances. They are probably right next to us!

Stress occurs when we perceive (true or not) that we are unable to take control of our life. To prevent stress from taking its ugly toll, we sometimes simply need to take a break or deep breath and allow our mind and body to get it together.

Dr. Hans Seyle stated, "Stress is the wear and tear on your body caused by life's events." It is sometimes caused by unrealistic expectations of others and of self. Also, much stress is brought on by a person's inability to adapt to any given situation, especially when we don't know what our reaction is expected to be by others.

It is a fact that into each life some stress will come. Our job is to not allow it to be the boss. One of the most effective ways to combat stress and its army of side effects is to look for ways to slow your life down and not allow the hustle-bustle of everyday living to take control. Over-committing can cause stress even in un-stressful situations, so we need to learn how to say "No" to even some of the good things that come our way.

Into each life some stress will come.
Our job is to not allow it to be the boss.

One of the worst side effects of stress is the harm we do to those we love by our words and actions. When stress is in control, we say things we wish we could take back as soon as they leave our lips, but by then the harm is done. When stress is in control, we are not! We will do and say things that we would not do or say under normal conditions. This can stretch relationships, sometimes beyond the breaking point. To have an understanding spouse during such situations is a blessing indeed.

Stress is lessened when we allow ourselves to accept the fact that we will make mistakes, and then forgiving ourselves. I think the best antidotes for stress are to think kind thoughts and do kind deeds. If we can force ourselves to look for ways to help others, we will find our own stress levels decrease. I have also discovered that stress backs off when we concern ourselves with the business of today and not allow our thoughts to take us to days gone by or days to come. Matthew 6:34 tells us, *"Therefore do not worry about tomorrow, for tomorrow will worry about itself. Each day has enough trouble of its own."* To lessen the stress of today, don't take the worries of tomorrow to bed with you.

Here's a list of six steps offered by the **National Mental Health Association** to help relieve stress that I want to share with you:

> 1.) Talk it out, don't bottle it up.
> 2.) Escape for awhile. Find a quiet place to relax.
> 3.) Work off your anger (do something constructive/physical)
> 4.) Do something for others.
> 5.) Take one thing at a time.
> 6.) Shun the "Superman" urge. No one's perfect.

Ironic I know, but if I were completely honest with you, I would have to admit that I have placed a certain amount of stress on myself by writing this book and from trying to meet a deadline to get the finished product off to the publisher. Maybe this chapter was written for me more than anyone else. There I go again, worrying about what lies in the future! A good rule to live by is this: Don't be stressed about the future until you have learned to manage the present because I think we would all agree, *stress is a mess!*

*****

Do not be anxious about anything, but in everything, by prayer and petition, with thanksgiving, present your requests to God.
[Philippians 4:6]

I Lost, But I Won!

Y ou might be saying, "I wish you would make up your mind. Did you win or did you lose?" My answer would be, "Yes." Because the truth of the matter is, we can actually lose at whatever it is we are attempting, but if we gave our all and held nothing back, then in a real sense, we won. For success should never be measured against what someone else has done or can do. It is always a personal victory. When you know without any doubt that you gave your best, you have earned the right to hold your head up high.

To achieve the status of success means fulfilling your role in the society in which you live. Remember, true success has nothing to do with what others think of you, but in knowing that you gave your all. If you have given your everything and the world demands more, pay no attention to the foolishness of it. Give your best, no matter what. If the world does not recognize or reimburse accordingly, the next time you have the opportunity to visit the neighborhood, do your best again!

"Give your best no matter what."

It has been said that success is setting aside eight hours each day for working and eight hours each day for sleeping. The success part comes in when you make sure they are not the same eight hours! Even at that, we still have eight hours remaining in each day for fulfilling the required duties of just being you.

Sometimes success moves slower than we would like. We must realize that success is achieved more often with small steps than giant leaps. Benjamin Franklin said, *"To succeed, jump as quickly at opportunities as you do to conclusions."*

One man's success might be failure to someone else. Success is determined by doing the best you can with what you have. It is in the realization that you have used all your resources to overcome resistance. Success is determined by the distance between where you started in life and where you ended.

As long as a person has used all his ability in all the best ways he knew how, to make the world a little better, I dare anyone to call him a failure. For that, my friend, is the epitome of success.

Everyone, young and old alike, owes it to himself and to the world to do the best he can. For to have the ability to do a certain thing and then not to do it when the opportunity presents itself is to fail. However, to the one who has given his all, the world stands in awe.

It is a fact that few people can achieve success without having the right players on their team. Occasionally, we will be in the right place at the right time to claim success. However, we must not allow ourselves to fall into the habit of thinking it was anything more than luck.

No one has the right to expect a person to do more than he or she can. It has been shown many times that if you give your best, you will receive the best in return. If you give less than your best, you will receive the leftovers. Success does not mean that we have to do it all, but it does mean that we have to give it all!

**"If you give less than your best,
you will receive only the leftovers."**

If our daily prayer were, *"Lord, help me to be all I am capable of becoming,"* the world would be a different place indeed. When we find our life on earth coming to an end, may we look back and smile, knowing we have done our best and fulfilled our duty. For if you sow the best seed you have, you will reap a harvest that you can be proud of.

One of my favorite writings on the subject of success is by Ralph Waldo Emerson, and I would be remiss if I did not include it, so here it is: *"To laugh often and much; To win the respect of intelligent people and affection of children; To earn the appreciation of honest critics and endure the betrayal of false friends; To appreciate beauty, to find the best in others; To leave the world a bit better, whether by a healthy child, a garden patch or a redeemed social condition; To know even one life has breathed easier because you have lived. This is to have succeeded."*

As one can tell, there are many ways to succeed in life, but all include the art of touching another life for good. Each of us has the ability to do so, and when we can lie down at night with the assurance that we have fulfilled that role, we can claim success.

**"Success is the result of trying,
not necessarily ending in triumph."**

Success is the result of trying, not necessarily ending in triumph. However, if it does, that can be considered a bonus!

*****

"Do not let this Book of the Law depart from your mouth; meditate on it day and night, so that you may be careful to do everything written in it. Then you will be prosperous and successful." [Joshua 1:8]

Just Trust Me On This

~:~

Have you ever heard someone say, *"Just trust me on this,"* and your guard automatically went up? Why? Probably because you have been burned too many times and are determined not to let it happen again. However, there is scientific evidence that indicates that people with trusting hearts have a tendency to live longer and healthier lives.

Almost everyone knows that people who have "Type A" personalities seem to be less patient and are more easily moved to anger and hostility when dealing with others. Where does the anger come from? Scientists say it stems from a skeptical mistrust of others. They say that when we believe others are going to mistreat us, they usually do. So, for your own good, *"Just trust me on this."*

"Trust everyone until they give you a reason not to."

I believe it is far better to trust everyone and be taken advantage of than it is to trust nobody and go through life without friends. As a matter of behavior, I think it is wise to trust everyone until they give you a reason not to. There is an old saying, *"Skin me once, shame on you. Skin me twice, shame on me!"* We owe it to ourselves and others to offer trust until it has been broken. Then we owe it to ourselves and others to take caution. If we continually allow others to take advantage of us without confronting them, we do an injustice to everyone involved.

It is far better to be deceived than to deceive; your life will be fuller if you occasionally get taken by trusting others than it would be if you trusted no one. Knowing that you may be taken advantage of, yet being willing to trust others is the foundation of civilization. However, I can assure you that you should put more confidence in a person's character than in the words they speak. For words deceive on a regular basis whereas character cannot tell a lie. In other words, trust little of what you hear and most of what you feel. The tough part is learning to assess the true character of another; you can't do this until you extend at least a certain amount of trust to them.

When it comes to building relationships, I believe **trust** is the most important part of the process. If we hope to have a relationship that will last through the good times and the bad, we must make sure trust is built in. It doesn't matter if the relationship we're talking about is one of intimacy or business dealings, when there is no trust, there is no depth and it will wilt and die at the first sign of trouble.

You can encourage and build confidence in another by trusting them. On the other hand, you can discourage and destroy another by doing something to break the trust they extended to you. Trust is found by being trustworthy and lost by being deceitful. Trust too much and you will be deceived, but trust too little and you will be duped or disappointed. May you develop the ability to trust just the right amount so all will benefit.

**"Trust is found by being trustworthy,
and lost by being deceitful."**

Be the kind of person that your friends would trust enough to play chess with over the phone. Trust like that takes time, but the rewards will far outweigh any investment made.

Having others trust you will hold you responsible for your performance - your reputation is on the line. If you tell someone that you will do something, you need to make every effort possible to do it or the level of trust they have in you will go down. If you find out that you have over-extended yourself and are not going to be able to fulfill a promise you made to someone, get in touch with them immediately and let them know. This will do much to keep your trustworthiness in place.

I have seen a sign in a number of eating establishments that reads, *"In God we trust. All others are on a cash basis!"* If we want people to trust us, we have to pay our dues, so to speak, and prove ourselves trustworthy. I believe, though, the ones to whom you extend trust usually become trustworthy. No matter if they do or not, it is better to be the recipient of wrong than the giver of wrong.

To be trusted is to be loved, and to be loved is to be trusted. It is hard to separate love and trust because they go together like a hand and a glove. One without the other cannot fulfill its full potential.

Worry is the enemy of trust just as trust is the enemy of worry.

Worry is the enemy of trust just as trust is the enemy of worry. We must let go of worries to grab hold of trust. Without trust, little action is taken, and without action nothing is accomplished. Those who trust more try more and, therefore, do more!

Just a word of caution in regards to the person who praises everyone and everything; give them little trust. In most cases, they are just telling people what they think they want to hear rather than the truth. I know you may not believe that, but *just trust me on this!*

*****

Trust in the Lord with all your heart and lean not on your own understanding. [Proverbs 3:5]

The Truth Of The Matter Is...True.

ᵕ:ᵕ

Have you ever known someone who was so good at telling lies that they believed them themselves? The problem with being around someone like that is that you have such a tough time knowing what to believe and what not to believe. The conclusion that I have arrived at is not to believe anything they say, and wait for a more reliable source. I have also grown weary when people say, "The truth of the matter is...", because most of the time what follows is anything but the truth. If they have to identify it as "truth" for you, it probably has some ingredients of falsehood. No matter how you say it, *"The truth of the matter is true,"* or it is not truth at all.

It doesn't matter how much you stretch it or distort it, the true part of truth is still true. It may be looked upon as good, bad or ugly, but that does not change the fact that it is still what it is, truth. You may not like it, and that is OK; it is going to be what it is going to be! It makes no difference at what angle you look at truth, every facet will shine just as bright. Truth today has taken on the appearance of a precious jewel. It has always been such, but much rarer today. You can do your best to disguise a lie as truth, but that does not make it so.

If you always tell the truth, you don't have to rely on your memory to get you out of trouble. The fact is that even if you always tell the truth, some will still call you a liar. That is because they are not hearing what they want to hear, what they desire the truth to be. The truth and the perception of the truth are different, and acting on what we perceive to be the truth will lead to erroneous behavior. When what we believe to be the truth is actually not, it doesn't matter how logical our reasoning is, we will still be wrong.

The unwise act as if they are deaf and cannot hear the truth. If they would just open their eyes, they could see, even if they cannot hear, what the truth is. The reason it is so difficult to recognize the truth is that lies disguise themselves in such a way that you mistake them for what is true. Just because a majority believes what has been said does not make it the truth anymore than you standing in a garage will make you a car.

Just as surely as we must make regular visits to our dentist to prevent "tooth decay," we should self examine our words to detect any "truth decay," for that causes much more pain in the long run.

It is more difficult to defeat a half-truth than a whole lie because it just sounds more reasonable. It is not that some people mean to tell a lie, it is just that they have a tendency to remember big. And some would rather tell you the truth a half dozen different ways than to ever tell you a lie. I continue to struggle with how to differentiate.

"You have no need to defend the truth, for it will defend itself."

A person who always speaks the truth may not always live a life of ease, but he can lie down at night and not worry about the effects his words have had on anyone. Telling the truth will in no way tarnish your record, but lies can leave gashes that will never heal. Sometimes speaking the truth carries more dreadful consequences than telling a lie-but tell the truth anyway. If there is ever a question in your mind about whether to tell the truth or a lie, choose truth every time!

Anytime an argument arises and truth is the opponent to falsehood, truth will win every bout if it does not give up and throw in the towel. You have no need to defend the truth because it will defend itself. The truth may not capture your attention, but a lie will enslave the entire body. Always remain true to yourself and to what you believe to be true, and then you can hold your head high.

We always have a choice whether to tell the truth and be lonely, or err on the side of the lie and have plenty of company. I would rather be robed in the plain truth than to be voted "best-dressed" in a tuxedo with tales.

Sometimes the truth is hard to handle, and may best be presented later. However, it should never be sugarcoated with anything just to make it easier to swallow. When we must share the painful truth with someone, we should do it with gentleness, and only share as much as needed to get the desired results. Remember that we are under no obligation to speak the truth if we have not been invited to speak.

Truth contains wisdom just as a lie has folly. Truth is a narrow, one-way street that does not allow U-turns. If you make a mistake and cannot bring yourself to admit it, this is a sure sign that you value your reputation more than you value the truth. Real power is revealed by how truthful one is, not by carrying a big stick.

"Truth contains wisdom just as a lie has folly."

Time will erode a lie to the nothingness it is, but truth will stand tall through the trials of time. Sometimes people act as if they believe truth will run dry if used too much, and therefore they just sprinkle it about rather than pouring it on. Nevertheless, it truly does not matter if you sprinkle it or pour it, *"The truth of the matter is …true!*

*****

"Then you will know the truth and the truth will set you free."
[John 8:32]

Look At What I Don't See!

I love the story about a small child in a Sunday school class who was asked to draw a picture of what made her happy. After a few minutes of intense work by the youngster, the teacher happened by and asked what she was drawing. She replied, "I am drawing a picture of God." The teacher was intrigued by the idea, but said, "Nobody knows what God looks like." The little girl never ceased to draw but simply answered, "They will when I'm finished!" Oh, for each of us to have the vision of this child. We need to look beyond what we can see, and focus on what we can imagine. Therefore, I invite you to come with me, and *"Look at what I don't see!"*

A Chinese proverb says, *"If your vision is for a year...plant wheat. If your vision is for ten years...plant trees. If your vision is for a lifetime...plant people."* We need to make every effort to allow our visionary power to grow to the point of seeing past the obvious to the possibilities, not only in our own lives but in the lives of others as well. Our visions determine and define our life, and touch the lives of those who come under our care. A vision is no more than a promise of what is possible, and we must make sure that ours is not dimmed by the clouds of doubt we sometimes allow to gather.

Vision is brought to life through faith and the belief that there is always more to the picture than what is being seen. Where no vision exists, there is nothing to live for. Whatever you can dream, you can do if you will simply begin and not stop until your dream becomes real. We must have a vision of where we are going, or we will never know when we arrive.

"Where no vision exists, there is nothing to live for."

We must not allow the busyness of life to prevent us from planning for the future. So many times, we are so caught up in solving the problems of today that we overlook the possibilities of tomorrow. We should remember the past but utilize those memories to help us avoid the same mistakes in what lies ahead. Putting vision to work for us is dependent both on knowing where you are and where you want to go. Any vision not acted upon is useless. Joel Arthur Baker says it this way, *"Vision without action is merely a dream. Action without vision is just passing the time. Vision with action can change the world."* We must claim ownership of our visions, and make sure they show up to work everyday.

A vision is simply an instrument that allows you to see past where you are, to where you wish to be. It offers you the options available to make the trip a pleasant journey. It also provides a reason to "go" when the world says, "stop."

Guard your visions and your dreams from those who are out to make sure you "Don't do anything stupid!" Without the valuable lessons you learn from your mistakes, your visions will remain unattainable. Your visions are the foundation for your future life; make sure they are worthy of building on. To have a vision does not mean that you know exactly how it will all take place, it just means you know it can and will happen. The rewards of tomorrow are the results of today's visions.

"No guts, no glory!" The brave are those who look past all obstacles in the pathway to their vision, and march headlong into battle. It is not enough simply to have a vision; we must also be able to communicate it with those who can help us achieve it. For few visions ever come to fruition solely from the efforts of one person. For leadership to be effective, it must create a vision, share the vision, and lead the way in taking the necessary steps for it to become real.

"The rewards of tomorrow are the results of today's visions."

Visionaries have the ability to see past the ordinary of today to the extraordinary of tomorrow, and to see the possibilities rather than the problems. Nevertheless, visionaries must be careful not to allow complacency to take up residence in their dream house, for if they do, they become lazy and settle for far less than what is available. A visionary and a fool can look at the same thing and both see something entirely different.

One of the dangers in achieving a goal or vision is to become satisfied with the current accomplishment and not begin planning the path to the top of the next mountain. We limit the size of our world when we limit the scope of our dreams. The more you think you can, the more you can!

Vision has nothing to do with the eyes we *see* with, and everything to do with the eyes we *look* with. Stevie Wonder once said, *"Just because a man lacks the use of his eyes doesn't mean he lacks vision."* A man only has the capacity to receive what he can perceive. Never allow a dwarfed vision to cause you to live the life of a midget. Dream big!

"Never allow a dwarfed vision to cause you to live the life of a midget; dream big!"

Having a vision and the courage to act on it will bring great joy. A vision is nothing more than seeing things as you would like them to be, instead of the way they are. However, for a vision to become reality, the end must be visible from the beginning. From an old family recipe, I discovered that *imagination* is the main ingredient in the recipe for a vision worth devouring.

Helen Keller once said, *"What is worse than being born blind? To have sight and no vision."* Now I have no doubt that you have sight, so come here and *"Look at what I don't see!"*

*****

"In the last days, God says, I will pour out my Spirit on all people. Your sons and daughters will prophesy, your young men will see visions, your old men will dream dreams." [Acts 2:17]

LaVergne, TN USA
19 August 2010
193908LV00003B/2/P